"While the world, inclu _____ siren song of happiness a _____ Davis reminds us what the _____ _o. true contentment can only be found _____ _...ist. This book is powerful. It is needed. And it is so biblically relevant in a world that desperately needs this message."

Thom Rainer, president and CEO, Church Answers;
author of *I Am a Church Member, Autopsy of a Deceased Church*, and *Simple Church*

"In the 1640s, Jeremiah Burroughs wrote an extraordinarily influential book titled *The Rare Jewel of Christian Contentment*. Andrew Davis has written his own book—this is not a mere update of a Christian classic—but its theme and stance are similar. In a world characterized by so much discontent, some of it serious and some of it laughably trivial, the virtue of contentment is a rare treasure. Contentment in Christian perspective must never be confused with mere stoicism, proud self-denial, determined self-sufficiency, or condescending aloofness. Rather, it is the product of knowing Christ so well, and trusting him so fully, that the vicissitudes of life, no matter how dire, cannot hold a candle to the joy of steadfastly trusting our heavenly Father. This is a book to savor and reread, and then pass on to others."

D. A. Carson, research professor of New Testament,
Trinity Evangelical Divinity School

"Andy Davis's meditations on Scripture are always a gift to the church. This new book is no exception. Davis unpacks Scripture's teaching on contentment in a way that is pastoral and theologically faithful. Let this book guide you to a deeper faith in the gospel and a richer experience of contentment and hope in God's providence."

R. Albert Mohler Jr., president, Southern Baptist
Theological Seminary

"Years ago I was profoundly impacted in reading Jeremiah Burroughs's *The Rare Jewel of Christian Contentment*. It felt like I was being discipled in a major dimension of the Christian life I had barely heard about by a Christian from another generation. Burroughs is truly among the best of the Puritan writers. I was even more excited when I saw that Andy, a thoughtful pastor, profound thinker, and great communicator, had taken up the task of reexpressing this essential and powerful Christian truth for a contemporary audience. If there was ever a time a distracted and exhausted church needed this message, it is today. Burroughs's book became a classic for a reason. I think Andy's book will become a classic for the same."

J. D. Greear, pastor, The Summit Church, Raleigh-
Durham, NC; president, Southern Baptist Convention

"I had never heard of the Puritan pastor Jeremiah Burroughs or his work *The Rare Jewel of Christian Contentment* until I was asked to read this book by Andy Davis. That was my loss. Drawing upon this superb treatise and Scripture—in particular, the apostle Paul—pastor Davis leads us on a fruitful journey into the delights and blessings of finding true contentment in Christ. There is joy immeasurable to be found in Christ, and this book will help you find it."

Daniel L. Akin, president, Southeastern Baptist
Theological Seminary

"Andy has put his finger squarely on one of the biggest issues society faces today: we live in an age of discontent. I'm not talking about impatience or shrinking attention spans. There is a deeper, underlying ache in growing numbers of people that speaks to dissatisfaction and a resignation that life is not what it should be and that more is never enough. This problem plagues Christians and non-Christians alike, but for the believer, things can and should be different. Andy unlocks the keys to Christ-centered contentment and how we can align our desires with God's. Every believer will benefit from studying the principles and practices shared here."

Kevin Ezell, president, North American Mission Board,
Southern Baptist Convention

"I recommend everything Andy Davis has written. He is one of the godliest men I know. He not only believes what he writes; he also lives it. Both biblical teaching and personal experience flow from every page of this helpful, insightful, convicting, encouraging, and edifying book. I enthusiastically recommend it to everyone reading these words. It will deepen your relationship with Christ, increase your faith in a good and sovereign God, sweeten your sorrows, and put fresh resolve in your steps toward heaven. That's quite a claim, but I'm sure of it. You'll seldom read a more timely book than this one."

Donald S. Whitney, professor of biblical spirituality and
associate dean, School of Theology, Southern Baptist
Theological Seminary; author of *Spiritual Disciplines
for the Christian Life* and *Praying the Bible*

"Sooner or later everyone asks, Is there anything more to life? In this book, pastor Andrew Davis shows why. In vivid narrative and clear teaching, this book shows us the roots of our chronic discontent, no matter what we have or don't have, and then points us to the solution. If you think this book is a 'stop whining and be grateful' scold, you are quite wrong. Instead, this book shows us how to find contentment and, with it, something beyond contentment, joy. If you, like me, wrestle with discontent, then you will be glad you found this book."

Russell Moore, president, The Ethics & Religious Liberty Commission of the Southern Baptist Convention

"A gifted teacher explains, illustrates, and applies. Andy Davis is an incredibly gifted teacher who has given the church a 'jewel' with this book. Davis's treatment of contentment has challenged and encouraged my soul. It will yours as well."

Timothy K. Beougher, Billy Graham Professor of Evangelism and Church Growth and associate dean, Billy Graham School of Missions, Evangelism and Ministry, Southern Baptist Theological Seminary

THE POWER
of
CHRISTIAN CONTENTMENT

FINDING DEEPER, RICHER
CHRIST-CENTERED JOY

ANDREW M. DAVIS

BakerBooks

a division of Baker Publishing Group
Grand Rapids, Michigan

© 2019 by Andrew M. Davis

Published by Baker Books
a division of Baker Publishing Group
PO Box 6287, Grand Rapids, MI 49516-6287
www.bakerbooks.com

Printed in the United States of America

Library of Congress Cataloging-in-Publication Data
Names: Davis, Andrew M. (Andrew Martin), 1962– author.
Title: The power of Christian contentment : finding deeper, richer Christ-centered joy / Andrew M. Davis.
Description: Grand Rapids, MI : Baker Books, [2019]
Identifiers: LCCN 2018027341 | ISBN 9780801093883 (pbk.)
Subjects: LCSH: Contentment—Religious aspects—Christianity.
Classification: LCC BV4647.C7 D375 2019 | DDC 248.4—dc23
LC record available at https://lccn.loc.gov/2018027341

19 20 21 22 23 24 25   7 6 5 4 3 2 1

Contents

Part 4 Keeping Content

PART I

THE SECRET
of CONTENTMENT

FOLLOW CHRIST
JUST LIKE
Your MOTHER !!

one

A RARE JEWEL IN A DISCONTENTED WORLD

The stone had been formed in the depths of the earth centuries before it was found, transformed from worthless carbon by unimaginable temperatures and pressures. It had been driven to the surface of the earth by tectonic forces and had made its way down various tributary streams until it came to rest at the edge of the Abaetezinho River in Brazil. No one could know how long it was there, unrecognizable, covered with mud and sand. It looked like any ordinary stone, but it was precious beyond words. In 1990, a Brazilian farmer needed some water for his fields and stooped down to get it. The stone somehow caught his eye, and he scooped it up, dripping and dirty. There's no way the farmer could have known that he had just discovered the largest red diamond in history—13.9 carats in its rough form. All diamonds are rare, but red diamonds are the rarest of them all. That red diamond would eventually be cut into a triangular shape

11

weighing 5.11 carats. It is now known as the Moussaieff Red Diamond, after the collector who purchased it in 2001. Its sale price was undisclosed, but estimates put its value as high as $8 million.[1]

This amazing red diamond is exceedingly precious. An immeasurably more precious jewel to the Christian is *contentment*. In 1642, the Puritan pastor Jeremiah Burroughs preached a series of sermons on Christian contentment that were gathered and published in 1648, two years after his death. The title the editors chose was *The Rare Jewel of Christian Contentment*. It carries the reader through a powerful unfolding of this vital topic, beginning with the apostle Paul's assertion in Philippians 4:12, "In any and all circumstances I have learned the secret of being content" (CSB). Unfortunately, many Christians in the twenty-first century have never delved into the topic of contentment. Like the muddy rock scooped up from the bank of a Brazilian river, its true worth has been hidden from many eyes for centuries. I desire that more and more Christians would experience the kind of Christian contentment that Paul discovered and Burroughs so skillfully described. Its worth in eternity will prove far greater than that of the red diamond.

Why do I say that? Consider this hypothetical scenario: Imagine you just won the most extraordinary sweepstakes prize ever, but it came through supernatural means. Let's call it the "Faustian Travel Agency," owned and operated by a Mr. Mephistopheles.[2] The prize is a two-week all-expense-paid trip anywhere in the world. You will stay at the most expensive five-star hotels, eat the highest-quality food, cooked by the best chefs in the world. You will see the most spectacular scenery, drive the most expensive cars, and wear a whole new wardrobe specifically tailored for you. The trip will have the best of everything and will cater to your every whim.

But here's the catch: you would have to agree to be continually discontent at every moment of the trip. Would you do it? Two weeks of constant discontentment in the most luxurious setting possible? For many people, I think the answer might be pretty clear: "No way! Why would I want to be miserable for two straight weeks?" Actually, we see many of the world's most elite people essentially living out this kind of tragedy in real life—famous athletes and movie stars, living in spectacular mansions on their own private estates on rocky coastlines, with architectural plans that maximize the view of the sunrise or sunset over the ocean, yet tragically discontent, going from divorce to divorce, addicted to drugs, bored, even suicidal.

Conversely, suppose a different offer were made to you, this one by your heavenly Father. He is offering a painful trial of suffering. You will be publicly beaten, imprisoned in a gloomy dungeon with your feet in stocks. You will be deprived of food, water, medical care, and even light. Surrounding you will be other suffering prisoners, the stench of human bodily fluids, and the kind of despair that comes when the end of your agony isn't in sight. *But* you will also be filled with such a supernatural contentment through the presence of God that you will later remember it as one of the sweetest times of your life. And you will have the privilege of leading a whole family to Christ (see Acts 16:16–34).

Which offer would you take? If you are a Christian, it is possible you would choose the second experience, despite its high cost. And if so, you probably already agree that contentment is the greatest state of inner well-being one could ever have in this world. The value of contentment is vastly greater than any that the red diamond could bring. Yet despite the value of this rich, full, continual contentment, and despite the fact that it is possible for every Christian in the world to experience it, this exquisite jewel is rare in our lives. And how desperately the unsaved world needs Christians to discover it.

In this tragic world, we are surrounded by discontented people. Every minute of the day, it is possible to see evidence of this restless discontentment in the way people respond to circumstances. People show their discontent while driving, because the traffic is too slow. Or perhaps the weather is too hot, too rainy, or too humid. Or in their jobs people aren't making enough money or receiving enough credit for the hard work they are putting in. Or they can't stand their coworkers. People feel deeply disappointed with their marriage or with how their children are turning out. Their bodies are too fat or not beautiful enough. Mired in their discontent, people often buy things they don't really need to improve their outlook on life. People try to find their way into happiness by seeking healing from counselors for their dysfunctional childhoods. Discontent with the love they haven't found shows up in lustfully roving eyes at office parties. Their outlooks darken as they take the commuter rail to another day at the same jobs that have imprisoned them for years.

The restless discontent of the world of non-Christians will not surprise many believers who have sought to win them to Christ. We realize Scripture reveals the true spiritual condition of the lost: they are "without hope and without God in the world" (Eph. 2:12 CSB). They are "harassed and helpless, like sheep without a shepherd" (Matt. 9:36). Their enslavement to invisible powers of darkness (Eph. 2:1–3) means that they share with Satan and the demons the same restlessness that causes them to roam the earth, constantly seeking some kind of rest but finding none (Job 1:7; Matt. 12:43). The spiritual condition of the lost and their bondage to sin guarantees that they can never find true rest and peace, which are essential to genuine contentment. Isaiah put it plainly: "'The wicked are like the tossing sea; for it cannot be quiet, and its waters toss up mire and dirt. There is no peace,' says my God, 'for the wicked'" (57:20–21).

This churning discontentment of unbelievers explains a lot of the terrible events that happen on planet Earth. Powerful rulers, discontent with the size of their domains, move out in greedy conquest, leaving a bloody trail of death and destruction across the pages of history. Every crime that rips apart the fabric of society comes from discontent people who are addicted to drugs, alcohol, money, power, or sensual pleasure and are willing to destroy other people's lives to get what their restless souls are demanding. Every marriage that ends in divorce begins that tragic journey in a heart of discontent. Though we cannot say that every misery in this world begins with human discontent, we may safely say that all the suffering of the world is exponentially intensified by the failure to find genuine contentment in the midst of any and every circumstance.

As Christians, we should be surprised by none of this diagnosis of the unbelieving world. But the great tragedy is that so often we don't really seem to live much differently. Many Christians hardly ever experience the daily foretaste of heaven that the Holy Spirit lives within us to provide (Eph. 1:13). Many display high levels of discontentment in all the same circumstances that I just listed, and in countless others.

Many of us Christians are restless, searching for something of value in our lives and not finding it. Many are spiritually immature, unable to handle even the smallest afflictions and inconveniences without verbalizing our complaints to whomever will listen. Many Christians live such discontent lives that they are never asked by any of the similarly discontent unbelievers surrounding them to give a reason for the hope that they have (1 Pet. 3:15), because they don't evidently have any hope.

What makes this all the more amazing is that, for over two and a half centuries, developments in science, industry, the economy, and medicine have steadily and systematically reduced the physical miseries common to every preceding generation of humanity. The Industrial Revolution brought astonishing technological progress to the world, resulting in labor-saving devices, new sources of power, amazing advances in transportation, indoor plumbing, and houses wired for electricity. Heating and air-conditioning regulate the temperature that surrounds us at nearly every moment. Refrigerators enable us to keep perishable items fresher longer, and delivery systems from the farmland to our homes ensure that a constant stream of delicious and affordable foods will keep our families eating like royalty. Medical researchers never stop searching for remedies to ailments and diseases that make life so miserable. And we have a clear expectation that someone somewhere is applying technological genius to remove every painful affliction from daily life. We say, "If we can put a man on the moon, surely we can cure the common cold!" The digital revolution has been a miracle of modern science, and our amazing little smartphones bring the entire world to our hands instantaneously.

Yet despite all of these advancements, we are more discontent than ever. Gregg Easterbrook wrote a book on this very topic entitled *The Progress Paradox: How Life Gets Better While People Feel Worse*.[3] In First World countries, he argues, even as the advances I have just cataloged have materially improved the physical comfort level of everyone in those societies, the rates of depression and psychosis continue to rise. People feel their lives lack meaning, and they can't seem to find any remedy to the plague of their own consistent discontentment. A clear example is transportation across long distances. It has never been easier, and yet still we complain! I remember sitting recently in a brand-new airport terminal reading a historical account of the Pilgrims on the *Mayflower* crossing the North Atlantic in perilous conditions in November of 1620. These intrepid people lived for many weeks in the dark and crowded below-deck area, eating cold biscuits and putting up with the stench of the vomit caused by the incessantly heaving little ship. A woman even gave birth in that setting. As I was reading this book, I overheard a well-dressed businessman as he was walking by me, talking with immense annoyance on a cell phone: "Yeah, it was a total nightmare! We were sitting on the tarmac for over an hour before we finally took off! Now I'm probably going to miss my connecting flight!" His voice trailed off as he bustled past me, and I chuckled to myself about his perspective. He was certainly not thinking how blessed we are to be able to cover thousands of miles by air in the astonishing comfort of a modern jet. We don't have to board a tiny wooden sailing vessel and cross a terrifying ocean. Neither do we have to load up a Conestoga wagon with weeks of provisions and cross churning rivers without bridges in a perilous journey to the Oregon Territory.

Another factor in our present-day discontentment is that we are more aware of the general misery of the human race than ever before. Our smartphones link us to news apps that keep us up to date on major occurrences around the world, pouring a steady stream of human suffering into our consciousness. We are instantly aware of a devastating earthquake in the Indian Ocean and the subsequent tsunami that wipes out whole communities and kills thousands. Or we hear of yet another terrorist attack in London or Paris or Madrid resulting in the killing or maiming of dozens. Or we read about a virus for which there is no cure, originating in West Africa and threatening to spread by human carriers through air travel to metropolitan sites all over the world. We realize that this is a world of misery in which very few ever find lasting contentment.

It is in this pulsating, seething world of restless unhappiness that I desire to rediscover the rare jewel of Christian contentment—first from the Scriptures and then from Burroughs's masterpiece—and make its ancient light shine radiantly for the twenty-first-century reader. It has the power to bring supernatural peace and eternal fruitfulness into any and every circumstance we will ever face in life and is therefore much more valuable than Moussaieff's stunning red diamond. My thesis for this book is that Christian contentment is finding delight in God's wise plan for my life and humbly allowing him to direct me in it. My goal is that we will more consistently display Christian contentment so that, in the end, God will be glorified in our daily lives, we will be more joyful, we will be sources of inspiration, and those watching us will seek the Savior, through whom alone they can have this same supernatural contentment.

two

PAUL TEACHES THE SECRET OF CHRISTIAN CONTENTMENT

In the world of literature and movies, there are few themes that can captivate the imagination as powerfully as a secret treasure. English explorer Sir Walter Raleigh set out in 1595 to find a magnificent secret golden city called El Dorado, and though he never found it, he wrote in his account *The Discovery of Guiana* that he had come very close to discovering its location. His description was so vivid and his reputation so powerful that for centuries cartographers charting the New World put El Dorado on their maps near where Raleigh might have found it. In Robert Louis Stevenson's 1883 novel *Treasure Island*, there is a secret treasure map in which *x* marks the spot where the pirates buried their treasure chest. The 2004 action movie *National Treasure* focuses on a map encoded on the back of the Declaration of Independence that leads to an ancient treasure hidden below Wall Street.

My favorite story of a hidden treasure map comes from Alexander Dumas's classic *The Count of Monte Cristo*. In that powerful story set in the Napoleonic era of France, Edmund Dantes is unjustly imprisoned on the island of the Chateau d'If. He meets and befriends an old, eccentric but wise fellow prisoner named Abbe Faria. As Faria lays dying, he bequeaths to Dantes a rolled-up piece of ancient paper with some secret markings made in an ink that can only be revealed by fire. On this mysterious paper are clues to a mind-boggling amount of treasure buried on the small Mediterranean island of Monte Cristo. After Faria dies, Dantes escapes the prison, makes his way to Monte Cristo, and discovers the treasure, worth over eighty million francs. Dantes in today's values became an instant billionaire, all because of an old piece of paper.

As far-fetched as this may sound to us, Jesus actually likens the value of salvation to a secret treasure hidden in a field (Matt. 13:44). Christian contentment is part of that spiritual treasure. It has such transformative power that it is far more valuable than any physical treasure that has ever been buried beneath the surface of the earth. And the apostle Paul claims to know where the treasure of contentment is buried.

The greatest statement on Christian contentment in the Bible is found in Paul's Epistle to the Philippians. For us to discover the treasure of contentment, we must absorb the power of what he said twenty centuries ago: "In any and all circumstances I have learned the secret of being content" (Phil. 4:12 CSB).

Do Paul's credentials merit our full attention on this topic? I believe so! As I have studied the bloody trail of heroism that has characterized the advance of the gospel from Jerusalem to the ends of the earth, I know of no single individual who experienced more suffering than this man. And no other man attained such a clear understanding of Christian contentment.

Paul's Credentials

Paul's life of suffering as a Christian began on the day of his conversion: he was struck blind with the heavenly light of Christ's appearance to him on the road to Damascus. Christ said about Paul, "For I will show him how much he must suffer for the sake of my name" (Acts 9:16). In 2 Corinthians 11, Paul lists his credentials of suffering:

> [I have endured] far greater labors, far more imprisonments, with countless beatings, and often near death. Five times I received at the hands of the Jews the forty lashes less one. Three times I was beaten with rods. Once I was stoned. Three times I was shipwrecked; a night and a day I was adrift at sea; on frequent journeys, in danger from rivers, danger from robbers, danger from my own people, danger from Gentiles, danger in the city, danger in the wilderness, danger at sea, danger from false brothers; in toil and hardship, through many a sleepless night, in hunger and thirst, often without food, in cold and exposure. (vv. 23–27)

And yet this isn't even the complete story of Paul's suffering! There would be more time in prison and the enduring of afflictions not mentioned in the text of Scripture. As the final act, Nero executed him, likely by beheading. If you look carefully at the list above, it can overwhelm you. I have never been shipwrecked, but Paul was—*three times*. He spent a night and a day adrift in the open sea. Imagine the terror of treading water in darkness, seeking something floating on the sea to hold on to. He mentions his savage beatings in detail—five times with lashes, three times with rods. In Galatians 6:17, Paul says, "From now on let no one cause me trouble, for I bear on my body the marks of Jesus." Paul's scars on his back were a powerful testimony to the level of suffering he had endured for Christ.

Roman imprisonments were brutal. There was no concern for prisoner comfort, no plan for meals or for medical care, and no concern for a just and speedy trial. Paul's imprisonment in Caesarea went on for years. Paul had to wait patiently for his freedom, though he'd done nothing wrong. He'd made a personal connection with Felix, the Roman governor, who often summoned him to speak with him. After *two years* of this, Felix was succeeded as governor by Festus, but Felix left Paul in prison (Acts 24:27). His suffering continued.

It is so powerful when a person like Paul steps up to teach us life lessons on contentment. If he can be content in this level of agony, maybe he has something he can teach us. We can read Paul's credentials from the pages of the New Testament. But the Philippian church had personally seen Paul live out supernatural contentment firsthand, when he and Silas came to their city to preach the gospel.

The Second Greatest Display of Contentment in History

I can scarcely imagine a more heroic display of a Christian teacher practicing what he preaches than Paul in the Philippian jail. The account in Acts 16 is unforgettable. Paul and

Silas went to Philippi. There lived a demon-possessed girl who did some fortune-telling, making huge sums of money for her owners. But the demon drove her to follow Paul and Silas and harass them by crying out in a mocking voice, "These men are servants of the Most High God, who proclaim to you the way of salvation" (Acts 16:17). Finally, Paul had had enough. He turned and said, "I command you in the name of Jesus Christ to come out of her" (v. 18). Immediately, the demon came out of the girl and she was healed.

But instead of her owners rejoicing at her healing, they angrily bewailed their loss of income and seized Paul and Silas, dragging them into the marketplace to face the city's rulers. The rulers violently tore off Paul's and Silas's clothes and had them beaten with rods before all the people. It's hard to conceive of what such a whipping must have felt like physically. Their wounds must have been grievous, for later that evening the Philippian jailer immediately cared for those wounds as the first display of his conversion. Beyond the physical torment was the public humiliation of such a degrading beating.

Paul and Silas were thrown into prison to await what would come, which could mean anything from execution the next day to indefinite imprisonment. The prisons of the first century were barbaric. From the account, we know that their feet were restrained in stocks in the worst part of the prison. The stench of human waste must have been overpowering. The prison was in almost-total darkness. They had to listen to the groans and cursing and complaints and foul speech of the other prisoners. Their five senses were on absolute overload with the suffering—nothing of beauty for their eyes, ears, noses, tongues, or skin to sense. Furthermore, their immediate prospects were dismal, if not terrifying. No food, drink, or medical treatment on the horizon. Magistrates could have rid themselves of the problems associated with these two men with two simple executions. At the very least, they were likely to be beaten again.

Yet, despite this immense level of suffering, Paul and Silas broke out in songs of praise at midnight, worshiping God for the joy of their salvation. This may be the second greatest act of supernatural contentment in history; the only one that surpasses it is Christ's willing submission to his Father in dying on the cross "for the joy that was set before him" (Heb. 12:2).

And what was the outcome of their display of supernatural contentment? First, all the other prisoners were listening to them, mystified by this display of joy and peace regardless of circumstances. Perhaps some of them would soon come to Christ. Then God sent an astounding earthquake in which all the prison doors were opened and the prisoners' chains fell off. But no one was injured and no one escaped! The earthquake led the jailer to assume that all his prisoners had fled, which meant, under Roman law, that he would be executed for his negligence. He drew his sword and was about to commit suicide, unaware that his eternal soul hung over the pit of hell.

Out of the darkness, Paul's voice rang out to rescue him from death and hell: "Do not harm yourself, for we are all here" (Acts 16:28). The jailer called for lights, rushed into the inner cell where Paul and Silas were, and, trembling, fell on his face before them. Then he brought them outside into the night air and said, "Sirs, what must I do to be saved?" (v. 30). This is the most important question any soul can ask, and the overpowering combination of events that evening forced him to ask it right there and then. Paul's answer stands over all of time: "Believe in the Lord Jesus, and you will be saved, you and your household" (v. 31). Right there and then, this man came to saving faith in Christ. I personally have little doubt that Paul and Silas's supernatural display of Christian contentment was essential to his asking that question and, therefore, to his salvation.

Later in this book, I will develop more fully the evangelistic power of Christian contentment. It is no stretch to say that the Lord may orchestrate amazingly challenging circumstances for you and your family for the primary purpose of giving your supernatural hope and Christian contentment a platform. As despairing lost people look on and see a buoyant peace and joy that is not based on favorable earthly circumstances but rather on faith in Christ, they will ask "you for a reason for the hope that is in you" (1 Pet. 3:15). That hope shines most brilliantly when earthly circumstances are darkest, and the rare jewel of Christian contentment is a radiant source of that light.

Paul and Silas's experiences in the Philippian jail were essential to the founding of that local church. Paul says in his epistle to them that, from the very start, they partnered with him in the spread of the gospel (Phil. 1:5; 4:15). This was a love relationship forged in the fires of persecution, birthed through a tremendous display of Christian contentment.

Yet Christian contentment did not preclude Paul from fighting against the injustice of their being beaten without a trial, despite the fact that both Paul and Silas were Roman citizens. When the order came the next day to release them, Paul refused to leave quietly. He said to the magistrates' officers,

"They have beaten us publicly, uncondemned, men who are Roman citizens, and have thrown us into prison; and do they now throw us out secretly? No! Let them come themselves and take us out" (Acts 16:37). Christian contentment does not mean that we passively accept afflicting circumstances, making no effort to improve our situation. Neither does it mean laying down for injustice in this world. I believe that Paul was not merely sticking up for his own honor but was fighting for the religious freedom of this newborn church of Philippi. He sought to carve out some breathing room for them from the persecution they had already experienced and would experience again (Phil. 1:30).

Paul's Thank-You Note to the Philippians

This is the backdrop for Paul's Epistle to the Philippians. By the end of the epistle, Paul wants to thank them for money they sent for his support. But Paul can't merely say thank you. He is an apostle and a mentor in the faith for this church, and he wants to challenge them to grow in Christlikeness. Christian contentment is central to this. Here is the key section:

> I rejoiced in the Lord greatly that now at length you have revived your concern for me. You were indeed concerned for me, but you had no opportunity. Not that I am speaking of being in need, for I have learned in whatever situation I am to be content. I know how to be brought low, and I know how to abound. In any and every circumstance, I have learned the secret of facing plenty and hunger, abundance and need. I can do all things through him who strengthens me. (Phil. 4:10–13)

Paul asserts that his joy at their money is not because he had been in need (though he had been). Quite the contrary, he says that he has learned to be content whatever the circumstances. He was content in Christ before the money came; he will be content in Christ using their money for his needs; and he will be content in Christ after their money has been spent. He has learned the secret of being content, whether abounding in plenty or languishing in want; he knows how to be content at a lavish banquet and how to be content in a cold prison with a growling stomach. Effectively, he is saying their money will not improve the state of his soul in Christ the least amount.

He does not mean this in any way to insult them or their gift. He merely wants to use himself as an example in this matter of Christian contentment, as if he were saying, "You remember me! I am the man who planted a church by singing at midnight in your city jail, with an empty stomach and a bleeding back. If anything, I am even stronger now in Christ than I was then. The same secret of abiding, supernatural contentment is mine in Christ, and it can be yours."

Yet for all that, once the lesson has been given, Paul does clearly express his thankfulness to them for their kindness and generosity to him. "It was kind of you to share my trouble" (Phil. 4:14). He goes on to say that they have been doing this since "the beginning of the gospel" (v. 15), and he thanks them for renewing this pattern of generosity. But even here, Paul's thoughts soar above the bag of silver coins and the bread and blankets it will buy. His thoughts go forward to Judgment Day and to the eternity beyond. Their gift will be credited to their account in the books of the Lord, and they will receive an eternal reward from him on that final day (vv. 17–19). Paul is as deeply joyful about other people's rewards as he is about his own!

Yet Paul does not forget that they, as physical beings in this present world, will continue to have needs of their own. So in addition to striving after Christian contentment, they should know that the same God who provided so richly for his needs through them will supply all of their needs as well (Phil. 4:19). They will not be impoverished even in this present age by being generous as the Lord leads.

Let's zoom in on some key details in his words.

Christian Contentment: A "Secret" to Be Learned

Paul declares that abiding, supernatural contentment is a "secret" to be learned (Phil. 4:12), not part of the original equipment of conversion. Imagine a recruit to the US Army standing in line at boot camp, receiving his government-issued provisions as a new soldier—a stack of neatly folded clothing, topped off by a new pair of Army boots. Other things will be provided later. So it is with new converts to Christ: on the day of their justification, they receive full forgiveness of sins, adoption into the family of God, the gift of the indwelling Holy Spirit, a secure place in heaven, inclusion in the body of Christ, and so forth. But the secret of Christian contentment "in any and every circumstance" is not included in the original set of equipment.

So when Paul saw the glorified Lord Jesus on the road to Damascus and was then baptized into the Christian faith, the lesson of Christian contentment was yet to be learned. It was in the school of daily life, and especially in extreme suffering, that Paul would learn this priceless lesson. As Paul actually lived through a wide array of circumstances in service to Christ—from the bitterness of persecution to the sweetness of deep Christian fellowship—he learned and was "initiated" into the secret religion of Christian contentment.

Since this is a secret to be learned, two things are implied: (1) not every Christian has learned it, and (2) it *is* possible to learn. Many Christians, it seems, go through their entire lives struggling, fuming, fretting, murmuring, fussing, arguing, and complaining against God and against their life circumstances. Sadly, I have proven on many occasions that it is possible to be a genuine Christian yet sinfully discontent. And we might never learn contentment. However, it is possible to learn it as Paul did, to reach the level of sanctification where we are actually content "in any and every circumstance." That gives all of us on this pilgrimage of Christian growth a very real hope. If Paul can learn it, and if he is commending it to the ordinary Christians of Philippi, then we can learn it too.

Contentment Is Self-Sufficiency?

One of the most stunning aspects of Paul's teaching is the Greek word he uses,[1] which most English translations render as "content." The simplest translation of that word is "self-sufficient," as though Paul were claiming to have learned the secret of having enough in and of himself. This is especially surprising in light of 2 Corinthians 1:8–9, where Paul teaches that becoming weaned off self-reliance was one of the main purposes of the suffering he experienced in Asia.

Jesus also clearly taught against this prideful tendency we have to trust in ourselves: "I am the vine; you are the branches. Whoever abides in me and I in him, he it is that bears much fruit, for *apart from me you can do nothing*" (John 15:5).[2] This one statement should destroy all self-reliance or self-sufficiency in us forever. But if it is true that apart from Christ, we can do nothing, why does Paul use the term "self-sufficient" for the secret state he has achieved?

It is not a matter of determining to care for his own needs and not be dependent on anyone else. Though Paul asserts that it is important for Christians to work hard with their own hands and provide for the needs of their own families so they will not be a burden to others (1 Thess. 4:11–12), and though he claims that his own hands and hard work had provided for his needs and the needs of his companions (Acts 20:34), the assertion of providing for oneself hardly fits the context of Philippians 4. Why would he call it a spiritual "secret" that he has learned that applies to being well fed or hungry, living in plenty or in want?

So what does "self-sufficient" mean here? I believe Paul was speaking, at a much higher spiritual level, about learning to live a life free from any dependency on anything in all creation whatsoever. In this, he has learned the secret of being as free from creation as Almighty God is.

This brings us into the mysteries of the Godhead and an attribute of God called his "aseity." The most common way of speaking of this attribute is in terms of God's self-existence, the fact that God did not need to be created and draws nothing of his nature from anything in creation. Wayne Grudem calls it God's "independence," saying, "God does not need us or the rest of creation for anything, yet we and the rest of creation can glorify him and bring him joy."[3] John Piper gives us this helpful explanation of the aseity of

God: "Aseity refers to God's self-existence (*a*—from, *se*—oneself). God exists 'from himself.' God owes his existence and completeness as God to nothing outside himself. . . . God's act of creation was not constrained by anything outside him, nor was the inner impulse to create owing to deficiency or defect. . . . God does not need us or anything else outside himself to be God or to be happy. Creation does not complete God."[4]

Probably two of the best verses to support this doctrine are these:

> The God who made the world and everything in it, being Lord of heaven and earth, does not live in temples made by man, nor is he served by human hands, *as though he needed anything*, since he himself gives to all mankind life and breath and everything. (Acts 17:24–25)

> If I were hungry, I would not tell you; for *the world and its fullness are mine*. (Ps. 50:12)

God does not need anything from creation for his existence or well-being, for he existed before anything had been created. He does not need food or air or water. He does not need us to love him. He does not depend on our service, worship, faith, or obedience for anything in himself or for his kingdom.

This kind of independence from anything in creation is what is called an "incommunicable attribute" of God, for we are all created beings and depend on God for our continued existence. Yet there is an aspect of this independence of God that may be at the root of Paul's secret for abiding

Christian contentment. It could be that Paul is saying, "God needs nothing but God in order to exist and thrive as a being; nothing in creation needs to come in from the outside of God to sustain his existence. And I have learned to be like God in this regard; I need nothing other than God for my continued existence as well. God is God-sufficient, and so am I." Paul is saying not that he is self-sufficient but that he is *God*-sufficient!

Let's test this concept. You may well say, "Wait a minute! Didn't Paul have basic physical needs that were essential to his continued life?"

What would they be? Let's start in order of biological urgency: air, water, and food. Unlike God, didn't Paul need those things? Well, not ultimately. Suppose his air supply were entirely cut off. Medical science tells us the average person can survive for only three minutes without oxygen. How about water? The average person cannot survive much beyond three to five days without water. And food? The life-span without food is three to four weeks. Without these three substances coming into Paul's body, he would die.

But what then? Paul already addressed that: for him, to die is to depart and be with Christ, "for that is far better" (Phil. 1:23). If his air supply were cut off, he is no loser but actually gains infinitely: "For to me, to live is Christ, and to die is gain" (v. 21). From that perspective, all Paul needs, really *needs*, is Christ. Paul doesn't need the Philippians' money. He doesn't need friends to stand by him when on trial for his life—and ultimately, in fact, everyone deserted him (2 Tim. 4:16). He doesn't need to be esteemed by his own family or friends or fellow Jews—and again, in the end, they rejected him as they did his Savior. He doesn't need soft clothing, bodily health, honors and accolades, worldly wealth. He doesn't need to be noticed or thanked when serving a brother or sister in Christ. He doesn't need his personal freedom. There is not a creature or condition or situation on earth that is absolutely essential to his soul's well-being; Christ has made Paul a genuinely free man in regard to all these things.

God's independence doesn't mean that he doesn't derive pleasure and joy from creatures. He does. He delights in our praise, rejoices in our salvation, cherishes our sacrifices. In the same way, Paul can enjoy the creaturely world as well: fellowship with other Christians, the beauty of a spectacular sunset, the delights of a lavish feast, the peace of knowing that no possible enemies can attack or harm him tonight. These and all the other normal earthly blessings indeed bring pleasure to Paul's life. But he has learned to be as essentially independent of them as God is, to be as God-sufficient as God is.

C. S. Lewis put it this way: "He who has God and everything else has no more than he who has God alone."[5] It's as if the world and everything in it is nothing! And to some degree, Scripture asserts that this is true: "Behold, the nations are like a drop from a bucket, and are accounted as the dust on the scales; behold, he takes up the coastlands like fine dust" (Isa. 40:15).

The implications of this way of thinking are staggering. If we embrace that we have within our relationship with Christ everything we need for peace and joy at every single moment of our brief span here on earth, imagine how free we would be, in all our relationships, from self-serving clinginess or desperation. Or imagine how believing we have everything in Christ can help those of us who are married not dread losing each other by a sudden car accident or help those of us who are parents not fear the premature loss of our children. Even more generally, this belief frees us moment by moment from needing to be noticed, praised, or thanked whenever we do something worthwhile.

How many of us are tempted to give up serving in a marriage or church or work setting because those we are serving do not give us enough credit? Believing the secret that "I am God-sufficient and it is enough to know that God is with me and loves me" gives us a remarkable staying power in serving others.

"Any and Every Circumstance"

Paul says that the secret he's learned of Christian contentment applies to "any and every circumstance," including "plenty and hunger," as well as "abundance and need" (Phil. 4:12). The range of misery Paul faced in his Christian life was astonishing. He survived shipwrecks, public beatings, stonings where he was left for dead, and religious riots among zealous pagans at their temple in Ephesus and among zealous Jews at their temple in Jerusalem (Acts 19, 21). Some of his enemies took a solemn oath not to eat or drink until they had murdered him (Acts 23:12). He often went without food, and he experienced nakedness.

Conversely, Paul was richly blessed in many settings and was escorted into the highest circles. On the island of Cyprus, as a result of a miracle that silenced a sorcerer, the Roman proconsul Sergius Paulus embraced the truth of the gospel of Christ that Paul was preaching (Acts 13:6–12). It is easy to imagine that Sergius Paulus would have entertained Paul and Barnabas most lavishly after his conversion. The same was certainly true near the end of the book of Acts, when Paul was on the island of Malta. After the shipwreck, Paul miraculously healed the father of Publius, the chief official of the island. Luke records that Publius had an estate and lodged Paul and his companions there, entertaining them hospitably (Acts 28:7). Many others who were sick on Malta came as well, and Paul healed them all, whereupon Publius and the rest of the people poured out great honors on Paul and fully supplied them for their trip to Rome (v. 10).

In these settings at least, Paul would have sat in seats of honor at lavishly appointed feasts and would have eaten as much as he wanted of the finest foods. This is not to mention the rich hospitality Paul enjoyed in the homes of Christians all over the Roman world. Oftentimes these people so deeply loved Paul that they poured out affection on him and wept as the time came for him to depart (Acts 20:27–38; 21:5). It would be fully expected that Paul would have sat at table with these fellow Christians as an honored guest and dined fully on whatever they had to offer. And they would have offered their best.

These were the widely varying experiences in which the Lord worked this secret into Paul's life. Sitting in a stinking, dark prison cell with an empty stomach, Paul was enrolled in Christ's school of contentment. Sitting at a richly set banquet table, Paul was enrolled in Christ's school of contentment. For years, this secret had been woven into the fibers of Paul's soul.

The Secret? Strength from the Lord

Paul does not leave his readers wondering what the secret was: "I can do all things through him who *strengthens* me"

35

(Phil. 4:13). An abiding Christian contentment "in any and every circumstance" is an act of supernatural strength, like a spiritual Samson taking his stand in the field and striking down a thousand Philistines with the jawbone of a donkey, one at a time (Judg. 15:15). Our contentment is assaulted over and over by the three-headed monster—the world, the devil, and the flesh—that hinders every aspect of our Christian walk. The evil world system will consistently seek to pull our hearts away toward idols and lusts. The devil hates Christian contentment, and he unleashes wave upon wave of invisible flaming arrows of temptation to wound our hearts and drive us away from contentment. And our flesh responds shamefully and eagerly to these external assaults, opening the gates of our fortress to a besieging enemy. Thus a Christian must be a mighty spiritual warrior in order to stand firm in contentment. Proverbs 16:32 says, "Whoever is slow to anger is better than the mighty, and he who rules his spirit than he who takes a city." Winning these heart battles is as much a display of strength as anything ever done on any battlefield by any renowned hero of ancient times.

Throughout the centuries and from generation to generation, Paul has poured out this expert advice concerning abiding Christian contentment. The same secret is available to us now. As I've declared, Christian contentment is finding delight in God's wise plan for my life and humbly allowing him to direct me in it. Paul's example and discovery of this secret is a permanent treasure for every Christian.

PART 2

HOW *to* FIND
CONTENTMENT

three

THE DEFINITION OF CHRISTIAN CONTENTMENT

What kind of courage does it take to be the crown jeweler to King Louis XIV of France, to be handed the largest and most exquisite diamond you will ever see in your life and commanded to use all your skills to cleave it, grind its facets, and polish it to perfection, when you know there is punishment for imperfection? That was the task assigned to Sieur Pitau in 1673. The gem on which he was to stake his life came later to be known as the Hope Diamond, but at that point in its history it was called the Tavernier Blue, named for the French gem merchant who had obtained the uncut gem in the Guntur District of Andhra Pradesh, India. In its rough state, the diamond was massive, over 115 carats in weight. Even more spectacular was the intense steely-blue color that Pitau's skillful faceting would draw forth. Imagine him holding his breath as he cleaved that once-in-a-lifetime stone and reduced it to 67⅛ carats![1] I feel a little like Pitau right now as I seek to cleave apart the dense definition of Christian contentment first penned by Jeremiah Burroughs in 1642. Typical of the Puritans, it is long, wordy, and carefully crafted, packed with theology, needing explanation.

Contentment Is Commanded

Let's start with this simple truth: God commands every Christian to be content: "Keep your life free from love of money, and *be content* with what you have, for he has said, 'I will never leave you nor forsake you'" (Heb. 13:5). Burroughs put it this way: "To be well skilled in the mystery of Christian contentment is the duty, glory, and excellence of a Christian."[2] Because it is commanded, we are obligated to do it. Actually learning the secret of Christian contentment is the mark of a fully mature Christian, but even a new believer should immediately pursue it.

It is the duty of all Christians to strive after contentment every single day for the rest of their lives on earth. We owe this to Christ. A convicting question stands over all our moments of complaining discontent: Has Christ, crucified and resurrected on your behalf, done enough to make you content today . . . or must he do a little more?

Contentment Defined

So it may be that we are now fully persuaded that we must constantly pursue contentment. But what are we pursuing? Here is Burroughs's definition: "Christian contentment is that sweet, inward, quiet, gracious frame of spirit, which freely submits to and delights in God's wise and fatherly disposal in every condition."[3] This definition is very dense, as Burroughs himself acknowledged when he compared it to a box of precious ointment that needs to be broken open and administered for its full effect. Let's break it into three main concepts: (1) frame of spirit (mindset); (2) God's disposal (God's wise decisions about our lives); and (3) free and delighted submission (fully embracing what God has chosen for you). If you understand these three concepts, you will be able to comprehend Burroughs's full definition.

A Mindset

Christian contentment is a "frame of spirit," which means an attitude, or perhaps disposition or mindset. It is a way of looking at everything, a perspective. We could imagine the frame of a house—all the hidden two-by-fours and rafters and pillars that hold up the entire structure. The word "spirit" shows that it involves the whole of a person's inner nature, as we shall see.

Let's unpack the four descriptions Burroughs uses for this frame of spirit: sweet, inward, quiet, and gracious.

Sweet

Christian contentment is a sweet frame of spirit, a sweetness of disposition, outlook, mindset. As such, it is immensely attractive to others in this restless, weary, and sin-sick world of ours. Picture a fragrant magnolia tree on a warm spring day with a comfortable bench where someone is sitting, the breeze wafting through the flowers nearby bringing the delectable fragrance to your nose. What an inviting scene! A truly content Christian is like that tree: sweetly fragrant. People yearn to be around those with a sweet spirit. "Sweet" is often contrasted with two opposites: bitter and sour. All of us know people who are bitter or sour. We have no delight in any conversation with such people. The author of Hebrews speaks of a "root of bitterness" that can grow up and defile many (Heb. 12:15).

Bitterness may be thought of as looking backward nega- tively, and sourness as looking at the present and future nega- tively. A bitter person is usually suffering from unforgiveness toward others because of the way they've been hurt by them: "So-and-so did such and such to me." The bitterness pollutes their entire outlook. In some cases, the root of bitterness lies in a very great affliction—the death of a loved one, a chronic illness, a severe economic trial endured in the past. When the afflicted person cannot accept this as providence from God, bitterness ensues. In the book of Ruth, Naomi had lost her husband and both her sons to death. These were severe blows in her life, and she felt them deeply. Her name meant "pleas- ant," but she wanted it changed to Mara, which means "bitter."

A sour outlook is pessimistic about the future. Such people are always anxious, fretful, gloomy, negative, seemingly hopeless. How can a Christian be like that? We should be radiant with hope, fully expecting the future to be bright in the hands of a loving Father. But such people are like Eeyore of Winnie the Pooh fame:

> "Good morning, Pooh Bear," said Eeyore gloomily. "If it is a good morning," he said. "Which I doubt," said he.
> "Why, what's the matter?"
> "Nothing, Pooh Bear, nothing. We can't all, and some of us don't. That's all there is to it."
> "Can't all what?" said Pooh, rubbing his nose.

"Gaiety. Song-and-dance. Here we go round the mulberry bush."[4]

Inward

Christian contentment is heart work, deep and interior. Burroughs says, "If the attainment of Christian contentment were as easy as keeping quiet outwardly, it would not need much learning."[5] We are not enrolling in acting classes! We are not looking to "put on a happy face" while we are dying inside. I think of the well-known expression "the tears of a clown." When the comedic actor is in public, he laughs and makes others laugh with him. But alone, he weeps. Like comic genius Robin Williams, who spent a lifetime making the world laugh and then, on August 11, 2014, acted out on the sadness in his heart by committing suicide.

The fact that Christian contentment is a genuine heart state is what makes it such a rare jewel, and why it will take the rest of our lives to perfect it. Every Christian faces a massive and daily internal battle between the indwelling Spirit and indwelling sin (Gal. 5:17), and winning this battle is essential to Christian contentment.

Quiet

Christian contentment is a quiet frame of spirit. It is not tumultuous, roiling, churning, noisy, angry, raucous, riotous, murmuring, complaining, or stormy. It does not sinfully shirk duties because of a feeling of injury from God. It does not rise up and challenge God or become sullen and argumentative. In short, it is not rebellious. When Jesus would drive out a demon from a demon-possessed victim, the demon would often make the victim cry out, or writhe on the ground, or froth at the mouth, or throw himself into a convulsive seizure (see Mark 1:25–26). The demon does not delight in Jesus' power but is essentially in pure rebellion. He has been overpowered by Christ's infinite power, but he is enraged at it. Not so a Christian who is displaying contentment. Such a person is quiet under the hand of God, like the sea that stopped its stormy raging and became completely calm when Jesus said, "Peace! Be still!" (Mark 4:39).

This quietness is not passivity, nor complacency, nor is it opposed to various orderly forms of prayer and activity in the midst of trials. I will make that plain at the end of the chapter. But it does not pour forth worthless words of rebellion during hard times. A mature Christian learns to be as quiet as Job: "I am so insignificant. How can I answer you? I place my hand over my mouth. I have spoken once, and I will not reply; twice, but *now* I can add nothing" (Job 40:4–5 CSB). So we learn to put our hands over our mouths in severe trials and be quiet, watching and waiting in prayer to see what God will do.

Gracious

This word was used differently by the Puritans than we tend to use it. When we speak of a gracious person, we think of someone who is well mannered, acting with great social polish and politeness. Though we might think of this as a perfect description of Christian contentment, Burroughs means something far deeper than that. Christian contentment is a supernatural state that can only be achieved by sovereign grace working in cooperation with the human heart by the power of the Holy Spirit. Apart from the atoning blood of Christ and the regenerating work of the Holy Spirit, it is impossible. So also, apart from the ongoing work of abiding in Christ as a branch does the vine (John 15:5), it cannot be achieved even by a genuine Christian. Christian contentment is a work of ongoing salvation by grace through faith. It is not a natural temper or demeanor, like some mellow person who is "chill" about the things that are going on, laid-back, taking everything in stride. Neither can it be attained by willpower or by turning over a new leaf or by New Year's resolutions. In the end, Christian contentment is a miracle of sovereign grace working together with a regenerate soul. God will get the glory, and we will get the joy.

So, to sum up all these components, Christian contentment is a mindset produced by the sovereign grace of God in Christ, characterized by sweetness (not bitterness or sourness), genuineness from the heart (not acting or hypocrisy), and quietness (not murmuring or contentiousness).

God's Decisions about Us

Burroughs's phrase "God's disposal" is the theological center of Christian contentment. It is essential for us to understand and embrace it, or we will never be content in this pain-filled world. But the word "disposal" itself is perhaps unfamiliar to us. The word has to do with the sovereignty of God—God's gracious ordering of everything concerning our lives. Theologians generally call that the doctrine of providence, and it is so important that I will devote an entire chapter to it.

At this point, let's define "God's disposal" as God's decisions about you, your life, your world, and your future. Scripture reveals that God sovereignly rules over the tiniest details of his universe, including you and your life. The mystery of providence is so great because Scripture teaches that God in his omniscience and sovereign power made those detailed decisions about you before the creation of the world: "Your eyes saw me when I was formless; all my days were written in your book and planned before a single one of them began" (Ps. 139:16 CSB).

God decided when you would be born, who your parents would be, whether you would be male or female, how tall you would be, how naturally intelligent or athletic or outgoing. He decided what country you would be born in, what education you would get, what career you would have, who you would marry, how many children you would have, what things you would achieve, how long you would live, and when you would die.

When it comes to the gospel, he decided that you would be a Christian, who would lead you to Christ and when, who would train you as a Christian, what your spiritual gifts would be, what ministries you would be involved in, who you would also lead to Christ, and much more. All of these things are part of "God's disposal." Obviously these issues are very challenging for us to understand and to harmonize with human decisions and other factors. But this is the doctrine of providence.

President Harry Truman placed on his desk in the Oval Office a sign that said "The Buck Stops Here." The sign had to do with a saying that was popular in his day: "Pass the buck," which meant to shirk responsibility. Some government agencies were notorious for passing the buck, for failing to make decisions and take responsibility for them. When Truman said "The buck stops here," he meant, "As president of the United States, I am responsible. I will make decisions. And I will own up to those decisions." As an energetic and wise ruler, God has pondered the smallest details and largest themes of your life and has made comprehensive decisions about each one.

Burroughs calls it God's "wise and fatherly" disposal. This is unspeakably precious to us. God's disposals in our lives are perfectly wise. As Paul wrote in his amazing doxology, "Oh, the depth of the riches and wisdom and knowledge of God! How unsearchable are his judgments and how inscrutable his ways! 'For who has known the mind of the Lord, or who has been his counselor?'" (Rom. 11:33–34). Paul is almost speechless pondering the wisdom of God! He uses the word "depth." I picture Ferdinand Magellan in 1521, trying to measure the depth of the Pacific Ocean. He spliced together six lengths of rope that he had on deck, tied them to a cannonball, and lowered it to a depth of four hundred fathoms (about 2,400 feet). The rope wasn't long enough to reach the bottom. Magellan called the ocean "unfathomable," immeasurably deep. He probably would have needed more than fifty lengths of rope to hit bottom almost four miles down.[6]

God's wisdom is limitless, unfathomable. Not only that, but Paul calls it rich. It is a multifaceted, complex plan that God is unfolding in redemptive history. Paul also rebukes all human arrogance in thinking that we could know the mind of the Lord or serve as his counselor! We think we know best, but God's wisdom is far above us: "For as the heavens are higher than the earth, so are my ways higher than your ways and my thoughts than your thoughts" (Isa. 55:9). God's "disposal" in our lives is unfathomably wise.

"In every condition," God knows what will most achieve his glory and our blessedness.

When Burroughs speaks of God's "fatherly" disposal, he means that all of God's decrees concerning us are tender and compassionate, taking into consideration our needs, weaknesses, and conditions. As I meditated on this powerful word "fatherly," I came to admire what Burroughs chose to say. He could have chosen the word "kingly," as in "wise and kingly disposal," and it would have been theologically accurate. God is a king, and he sits on a heavenly throne and does whatever pleases him (Ps. 115:3). As his subjects, we submit to his kingly decrees and do not rise up against such a mighty potentate. But this image misses the tender, fatherly affection God has for us as his adopted children. God has put the spirit of adoption in our hearts, by which we cry out "Abba! Father!" (Rom. 8:15). His love for us is immeasurable. He is not a cold, calculating machine of providential decrees.

> Your Father knows what you need before you ask him. (Matt. 6:8)

> As a father shows compassion to his children, so the LORD shows compassion to those who fear him. (Ps. 103:13)

> You saw in the wilderness how the LORD your God carried you as a man carries his son all along the way you traveled until you reached this place. (Deut. 1:31 CSB)

> He arose and came to his father. But while he was still a long way off, his father saw him and felt compassion, and ran and embraced him and kissed him. (Luke 15:20)

No human father has ever shown greater tenderness or consideration or sacrificial love or deep affection for his children than God has for us. Everything that God carefully measures out and allows to come into our lives must first pass through the wall of his protective love. And when he brings pain into our lives, it is only to heal us and make us more glorious in eternity. Dr. James Dobson tells of a powerful moment when he took his three-year-old son, Ryan, to a pediatrician to have his ear infection treated. The pediatrician said that the infection had adhered itself to Ryan's eardrum and could only be treated by pulling the scab loose with a steel instrument. Ryan began to scream with pain and terror, and his father had to hold him down on the examination table.

> After hearing what was needed, I swallowed hard and wrapped my 200-pound, 6-foot-2-inch frame around the toddler. It was one of the toughest moments in my career as a parent. What made it so emotional was the horizontal mirror that Ryan was facing on the back side of the examining table. This made it possible for him to look directly at me as he screamed for mercy. I really believe I was in greater agony in that moment than my terrified little boy. . . . Though he was screaming and couldn't speak, he was "talking" to me with those big blue eyes. He was saying, "Daddy! Why are you doing this to me? I thought you loved me. I never thought you would do anything like this! . . . Please, please! Stop hurting me!"
>
> It was impossible to explain to Ryan that his suffering was necessary for his own good, that I was trying to help him, that it was love that required me to hold him on the table. . . . In his immature mind, I was a traitor who had callously abandoned him.[7]

Burroughs was so wise to use the word "fatherly." The word "kingly," however true, misses the tender affection God has for each of us. In the mighty decrees of a king, he does what is best for his kingdom. If that means sending thousands of soldiers to their deaths to protect the kingdom from an invading army, he will do it and still be thought of as a wise king. On the other hand, in the loving decisions of a father, he does what is best for his children. What is so amazing about providence is that the two are one and the same! What's best for the kingdom of heaven is also what's best for the children of God! We will see that far more clearly when we are in heaven.

Freely Submitting to and Delighting in God's Decisions about Us

Christian submission "freely submits to" God's wise and fatherly disposal. Submission involves gladly recognizing God's fatherly authority to make these kinds of decisions concerning his children. It means to yield, to place ourselves under, to bow down to our majestic God. The opposite of submission is rebellion, the essence of sin. By Christian contentment, we are embracing our role as creatures. Satan arrogantly rebelled in heaven and sought to take God's throne (Isa. 14:13–14). When Adam rebelled against God, he was following Satan's path of pride. Our salvation has as its essence bringing rebellious people back under God's kingly rule. Most of our restless discontent is nothing more than rebellion.

We are to submit willingly and without reluctance, not grudgingly or under constraint, as though we are being kidnapped, mugged, or enslaved. Job, in the height of his misery, felt himself completely powerless in the face of such a mighty God.

> How then can I answer him
> or choose my arguments against him?
> Even if I were in the right, I could not answer.
> I could only beg my Judge for mercy.
> If I summoned him and he answered me,
> I do not believe he would pay attention to what I
>   said.
> He batters me with a whirlwind
> and multiplies my wounds without cause.
> He doesn't let me catch my breath
> but fills me with bitter experiences.
> If it is a matter of strength, look, he is the powerful
>   one!
> If it is a matter of justice, who can summon him?
>   (Job 9:14–19 CSB)

Instead of feeling overpowered by this omnipotent God, Christian contentment submits willingly, freely, openly.

But Burroughs goes well beyond this free submission. For the crowning achievement of Christian contentment is that it *delights* in God's decisions in every condition! Our hearts become captivated by a supernatural, faith-filled perspective of God's glorious plan of salvation. We yearn to see King Jesus in his heavenly glory, surrounded by worshipers from every nation on earth (Rev. 7:9). We have come to learn that God's wise and fatherly decisions about us, even down to the tiniest detail, are essential to that eternally glorious end. And so, despite any temporary pain we must endure, we come to delight in all of it. Throughout the history of missions, godly men and women have gladly chosen to put themselves and their families in harm's way, knowing that it would most likely bring them pain. But they delighted in the outcome of their suffering and death, knowing it was instrumental in leading lost people to Christ. During the Roman persecution of the second century, a noble Christian woman named Felicitas boldly answered the Roman official who was interrogating her: "While I live, I shall defeat you. And if you kill me, in my death, I shall defeat you even more."[8] There is a sweet delight in the wise and powerful plan of God behind her boldness, and it gave her the joy she needed to be faithful unto death.

Because God's plan involves almost incalculable suffering for the people of God, the only way we can not only submit to but also delight in all the aspects of that plan is by faith in this future vision. We must imitate Christ's perspective of his own death on the cross, "keeping our eyes on Jesus, the source and perfecter of our faith. *For the joy that lay before him*, he endured the cross, despising the shame, and sat down at the right hand of the throne of God" (Heb. 12:2 CSB).

Putting Boundaries around the Definition

As he described Christian contentment, Burroughs wanted to make it plain that Christian contentment was not opposed to certain things.[9]

An Appropriate Sense of the Affliction

We are not in some kind of stupor, as though we are unaware of what is happening to us. Imagine someone who's been in a serious car accident and has yet to recover consciousness. He is heavily sedated, knowing nothing of what has happened to him or of how his future life will be affected. That is not a picture of Christian contentment. Rather, God would have us fully aware of our condition, and it is when we feel its weight the most that we can most glorify God in every condition.

An Orderly and Respectful Pouring Out of Our Complaint in Prayer to God

The book of Psalms displays the whole range of human emotions. And many psalms display the right way of "casting all your anxieties on him, because he cares for you" (1 Pet. 5:7). Under the inspiration of the Holy Spirit, the psalmists would say things like this: "Why, O Lord, do you stand far away? Why do you hide yourself in times of trouble?" (Ps. 10:1).

This is precisely what the Lord wants us to do with our emotions, struggles, doubts, and fears: to lay them at his feet and ask him to answer and resolve the circumstances. It is essential for grieving parents to cry out over the hospital bed of their dying toddler and ask God to heal her. It is vital for a single woman who yearns to be married to pour out her loneliness and hurt to her loving heavenly Father. It is necessary for an unemployed father of three who has been turned down in applying for twelve jobs in one week to cry out to God with his fears.

Lawfully Seeking Help and Deliverance

Christian contentment is not a stoic acceptance of hardship in this world, as though we are denying that we are in pain or that anything can be done about it. God does not delight in pain for pain's sake. The overwhelming majority of Jesus' miracles were healings, alleviating temporal sufferings in the lives of mortal people. He took very seriously the immediate physical needs of the people around him, including showing deep compassion for people who had been with him a long time with nothing to eat, fearful they would collapse from hunger on the way home (Mark 8:2–3). Jesus did not advocate merely accepting misery. We should seek treatment for our dying children, or a godly spouse in our loneliness, or a job that allows us to meet the financial needs of our family. Christian contentment has to do with our inner state before (and after) those prayers and efforts are answered.

Daily life is filled with aggravations and annoyances, and we are capable of alleviating many of those with reasonable efforts. This very morning, I found myself driving behind a dump truck that was moving extremely slowly. I was feeling pressure to get to my morning appointment and was continually looking for an opportunity to pass the truck. The theme of Christian contentment popped into my mind, and I chuckled to myself. "If you were really content, you would stay behind this truck even if it drove the entire way you are going! Even if it made you late for your appointment!" Then I saw the dotted yellow line on the road permitting me to pass. The way was clear and I comfortably passed the truck. Christian contentment is not a fatalism or a masochism that seeks pain for pain's sake. Christian contentment is finding delight in God's wise plan for my life and humbly allowing him to direct me in it. Jeremiah Burroughs's timeless definition is a powerful aid to us in our quest to walk in contentment in any and every situation we will face.

four

CONTENTMENT
AND PROVIDENCE

In the city of Dresden, Germany, there is a magnificent museum of the history of technology. In the summer of 2015, I had the pleasure of walking through its halls with my son, Calvin. Though there were many amazing exhibits of human ingenuity over the centuries, the most remarkable to me was a wristwatch made by A. Lange and Söhne called "the Grand Complication." I found out later that to buy this watch new would cost over $2.5 million and would require a full year for the skilled artisans of that company to complete. Each of its 876 individual parts is handmade, and even its interior parts are perfectly finished with meticulous precision.

The individual parts of this magnificent watch are of special fascination to me as a former mechanical engineer. I have watched several videos on how the Grand Complication is manufactured and have seen the artisans lift with tweezers a tiny metal part out of a compartment in a shallow rectangular box, study it with a jeweler's loupe, then place it carefully and move it precisely on a flat abrasive surface to polish it to within a ten-thousandth of an inch of tolerance.[1] Then, after that part is replaced into its compartment, the next tiny part is lifted out and polished as well. Each part is handled with the same meticulous precision until the entire watch is finished.

This is how I see the working of God in assembling the church of Jesus Christ over the centuries of redemptive history. The skillful watchmakers love what they do and take pride in making each part as perfectly as they can to fit into the overall design. So our loving heavenly Father works in each of his children's lives. Each person is shaped by each moment of time according to God's inscrutable purpose. Theologians have a name for the continual activity of God in the daily lives of his children: providence. Without a wholehearted embracing of the doctrine of providence, lasting Christian contentment will be impossible to attain. And the more vigorously we study, meditate on, and delight in the detailed providence of God, the easier it will be to grasp Christian contentment.

Not "Luck" or "Karma"

We need to learn to see the complexity of God's wise plan. We need to delight in his understanding of how the tiniest details fit into that plan. And we must see the hand of Almighty God in everything that happens in order to submit freely to it and delight in it. Otherwise, we could imagine "stuff" happening that seems so irrational, so irritating if it's minor, or so devastating if it's major. And God would be telling us, "I did not cause this; I had nothing to do with it. You'll have to make the best of it because there is no purpose behind it at all."

Mindless. Purposeless. Irrational. Some people use the terms "luck" or "fate." Others call it "karma." Unbelievers live their lives buffeted by the tossing waves of forces that seem to have no purpose whatsoever. When a tornado rips violently through a community, destroying some homes entirely, damaging others significantly, roughing some up slightly, and bypassing the rest entirely, it seems to them a metaphor for all of life. The storm blows through your life unpredictably, and no one can tell when it will come, how long it will last, or whether you'll even survive.

By contrast, the doctrine of providence sees a Person behind everything. There is purpose, intention, plan. There's a wise and loving Father behind every experience you walk through in life, every person you "chance" to meet, every bruise or cut you receive, every paycheck you earn, every flat tire you endure, every missed connecting flight, every possession that slips out of your pocket.

Providence Defined

Providence is the direct activity of God toward the universe he created, moment by moment sustaining its existence and overruling its events to cause the unfolding story of history to occur according to his will. Foundational to this definition is denial that the universe can exist for a single second without God's activity. When God created the universe, he did it in such a way that everything in it requires his constant active involvement for it to continue to exist. God created a needy universe. It has no separate existence, no possibility of independence from him.[2] If God so chose, the entire universe or any smaller part of it would simply cease to exist by his ceasing to uphold it by his invisible power. God could will Satan, any demon, or any human tyrant or criminal out of existence at any moment.

Beyond this, God works in a mysterious way, together with inanimate objects, animals, and intelligent beings (angels, demons, and humans), navigating their activities and choices to achieve his sovereign purposes without violating their freedoms. This is a stunning assertion, but it is clearly taught in the Bible (see Col. 1:15–17; John 1:1–3; Heb. 1:3).

The Marvels of Providence in a Messed-Up World

Every single one of the 876 parts in Lange and Söhne's Grand Complication watch is engineered to exact design specifications, such that the slightest imperfections would disqualify that part from the watch. Everything has to be as nearly perfect as human engineers can make it or the watch will not work. One of the designers speaks of how perfectly clean their laboratories must be, saying that even a single speck of dust might cause the timepiece to cease functioning properly.

This makes God's providential control of human history on planet Earth even more amazing. For when Adam sinned, God put both the planet and the human race under a curse, rendering both far from perfect (Gen. 3:17; Rom. 8:20–21). All human beings are born polluted with Adam's sin, deeply corrupted in both mind and body. We are all dangerously imbalanced. We are eccentric wheels, badly out of round. We are like gears with teeth missing, springs made from inferior metal, crystal that's been cracked and marred by a thousand scratches. The world we live in is just as defective, groaning under an endless cycle of decay and corruption (Rom. 8:22). None of this is a surprise to the sovereign Lord, who rules over every human being and every blade of grass.

And yet this is exactly the physical world and the human history that God causes to work together for our good and for his own glory. God orchestrates willful, wicked human beings who are irrational and erratic in their decisions to achieve every step of his sovereign purpose. God harmonizes a deeply flawed ecosystem, holding it together while advancing his wise plan to save his chosen people in every generation. The creation is groaning in decay and at the same time singing in harmony with his wise will. This absolutely boggles the mind!

In 1991, a zealous group of scientists launched an artificial closed ecological system in Oracle, Arizona. They gave it the hopeful name "Biosphere 2," because they were seeking to imitate Biosphere 1 (planet Earth) in its success. Its purpose was to show the viability of closed ecological systems to support human life in outer space. Designers had in mind human colonies on Mars, fully sustained within an ecological system that had everything it needed within itself. The ecotechnologists designed Biosphere 2 with a web of interactive systems, including an artificial rainforest, a miniature ocean with a coral reef, a mangrove wetland region, a savannah grassland region, a fog desert, an agricultural region for human farming, and a place for the eight humans to live. Despite the best efforts at balancing the oxygen, carbon dioxide, waste products, and cycles of life and death among its animals, birds, insects, and microbes, the whole experiment failed miserably. The oxygen level kept dropping steadily week after week, the fish died off rather quickly, and the populations of greenhouse ants and cockroaches exploded. Oddly, the morning glories overgrew the rainforest, crowding out other plants. The best thinking of ecologists and the investment of over $200 million was inadequate to create a healthy, balanced closed ecological system.[3]

Yet planet Earth (Biosphere 1), despite being cursed by God and subjected to futility in a cycle of decay and death, continues to make its defective way steadily toward God's preordained end. The cockroach population has not overtaken the world. The seismic activity of the earth's floating tectonic plates has not put an end to human life. The sun's radiation has not cooked us to death. The fish and plankton and algae and other biological species of the earth's oceans maintain their amazing balance. The rain cycle has continued, including the various weather patterns so well known to us. The seasons continue in their regular rhythms—spring, summer, autumn, winter—year after year.

And on this groaning and sin-cursed stage, a stunningly complex drama of human history unfolds, generation after generation.

Scripture Teaches the Meticulous Providence of God

Countless places in Scripture assert God's continual providential care over the universe. For our purposes, it's best to divide them into two main categories: (1) God's general care over the universe and its various creatures and (2) God's special care for the unfolding of human history, especially resulting in the salvation of his people.

The Bible begins with the famous words, "In the beginning, God created the heavens and the earth" (Gen. 1:1). Richard Sibbes says, "Providence is the perpetuity and continuation of creation."[4] The New Testament makes it clear that God is continually holding even the very atoms of the universe together through his Son, Jesus Christ: "In him all things hold together" (Col. 1:17). If God in Christ withdrew his energetic effort for a single instant, every atom in the universe would fly apart, would cease to exist.

The Bible reveals that God governs the continued existence and movement of the celestial bodies—the sun, moon, and stars. "Thus says the Lord, who gives the sun for light by day and the fixed order of the moon and the stars for light by night, who stirs up the sea so that its waves roar—the Lord of hosts is his name" (Jer. 31:35). The sun doesn't set accidentally or automatically, for God actually creates the darkness at the end of every day.

God's active, daily control extends to the distant reaches of outer space. Isaiah tells us that every one of the stars in the cosmos is named by God and sustained by God: "Lift up your eyes on high and see: who created these? He who brings out their host by number, calling them all by name; by the greatness of his might and because he is strong in power, not one is missing" (Isa. 40:26). This is astounding! Cosmologists estimate the total number of stars in the universe to be 1,000,000,000,000,000,000,000,000 (one with twenty-four zeros)! Each of those stars is named and sustained moment by moment by God. Isaiah applies that amazing knowledge to the people of God to cut off any complaints they may have that God has forgotten them: "Why do you say, O Jacob, and speak, O Israel, 'My way is hidden from the Lord, and

61

my right is disregarded by my God'? Have you not known? Have you not heard? The LORD is the everlasting God, the Creator of the ends of the earth. He does not faint or grow weary; his understanding is unsearchable. He gives power to the faint, and to him who has no might he increases strength" (Isa. 40:27–29).

Beyond that, God actively and energetically provides for the needs of all his creatures. There are literally trillions of living beings on planet Earth, and Scripture reveals that God feeds every single one of them every day: "The eyes of all look to you, and you give them their food in due season. You open your hand; you satisfy the desire of every living thing" (Ps. 145:15–16). The largest mammal on earth is the blue whale. It requires more than 1.5 million calories of food every day, so it is eating almost constantly. Its favorite food is krill (tiny shrimplike creatures), of which it can eat more than sixteen thousand pounds a day. Given that there may be as many as twelve thousand blue whales swimming the oceans, God has a massive job to do in keeping them all fed. But he does it every single day effortlessly. For nothing is difficult with God. And even the death of creatures is timed and orchestrated by God. When Jesus said that not a single sparrow falls to the ground apart from the activity of the Father (Matt. 10:29), he was speaking of their death. Jesus said, "Even the hairs of your head are all numbered" (Matt. 10:30). The infinite mind of God actually knows how many human hairs are still on the heads of over seven billion people all over the world.

Far more complex is the detailed management God exerts over the unfolding of human history. The doctrine of God's providence extends to the smallest details of a single human life and the largest extent of a worldwide empire. God has planned everything and is actively ruling every moment to make certain his plan is achieved. God spoke through the prophet Isaiah concerning the crushing defeat the Assyrians would suffer in Israel: "This is the plan prepared for the whole earth, and this is the hand stretched out against all the nations. The LORD of Armies himself has planned it; therefore, who can stand in its way? It is his hand that is outstretched, so who can turn it back?" (Isa. 14:26–27 CSB). "This is the plan . . . , and this is the hand." Almighty God made the *plan* before the foundation of the world; God's *hand* extends to every moment of human history to accomplish even the smallest details of his plan. And no one can devise a better plan or stop him from executing his plan.

The rise and fall of every nation is clearly part of God's wise and world-encompassing plan. "From one man he has made every nationality to live over the whole earth and has determined their appointed times and the boundaries of where they live" (Acts 17:26 CSB). That is mind-blowing when we ponder it, especially when we consider that the rise and fall of human empires always involved the most evil motives in the hearts of the conquerors. God holds each conqueror accountable for their actions, but uses their empires in his own inscrutable plan. God decided how long the Roman Empire would last and who would conquer it in the end. God decided where the Sioux, Pawnee, and Mohicans would roam in North America and when their boundaries would be curtailed by the European nations that would follow and settle down. God oversaw the rise and fall of the Spanish Empire in the New World, as well as the prosperity and duration of the Portuguese trading colonies in the Far

East. God decided that "the sun would never set on the British Empire" in the nineteenth century and that two world wars would end their worldwide reign in the twentieth. These powerful world empires were carefully planned out even before God said "Let there be light."

Just as remarkable are the details of history that lead to the rise and fall of whole empires. There is a well-known poem that captures the importance of the smallest issues that can decide the flow of human history:

> For want of a nail the shoe was lost.
> For want of a shoe the horse was lost.
> For want of a horse the rider was lost.
> For want of a rider the message was lost.
> For want of a message the battle was lost.
> For want of a battle the kingdom was lost.
> And all for the want of a horseshoe nail.[5]

God alone perfectly understands the vital importance of seemingly mundane events in changing the course of history. God has been seeing to the tiniest "nails" in every century, and he decides whether the necessary nail will be there at the critical moment . . . or not.

This grand, overarching plan extends to a single human life as well. Both the day of our birth and the day of our death were planned and written with indelible ink in the book of God's sovereign plan before we were born (Ps. 139:16). The details of our childhood and upbringing—who our parents were to be, their socioeconomic status, the places they would live, what their religion would be, how they would raise us, what education we would receive, what illnesses we would experience, who our friends would be, what words they would speak to us on a given Tuesday morning when we were fifteen years old—all of these facts and every other atomic detail were planned by God before one of our days began. Even the seemingly random events of inconsequential moments are controlled by the sovereign hand of God: "The lot is cast into the lap, but its every decision is from the LORD" (Prov. 16:33).

God controls the biggest events of our lives as well. The decisions we make concerning our occupations, our spouses, our children, our homes, our daily lives—all are woven into the fabric of God's complex tapestry. And it's not just our lives that are included but the lives of every other human being on the face of the earth. To revert to the mechanical analogy, the Grand Complication mechanism of this providential timepiece is beyond calculation. The Watchmaker crafted each tiny part just as he saw fit. He shaped the contour of a gear or an escapement or a pinion or a torsional spring to play its role in the movement of the watch. Because we are people with minds and emotions, we are continually wondering what the Watchmaker is doing as he heats us and bends us and drills holes in us and polishes us and puts us in place. We can scarcely begin to understand how our lives and free choices will interact with the billions of others on earth to achieve God's overall plan in redemptive history. But every moment is purposeful, and nothing is wasted.

God's Providence Means Salvation for Us, Glory for Him

God's purpose in ruling so meticulously over every atom of matter and every second of history is that he would be glorified in the salvation of his elect people. God orchestrates all these events so that not one of Christ's sheep will be lost, but every single one of them will be raised up on the last day (John 6:39).

In Ephesians 1:4 Paul makes it very plain that God chose us in Christ before the foundation of the world so that we should end up in heaven, holy and blameless in his sight. The apostle teaches that everything in this world is planned and controlled for his glory in our salvation: "And we know that God causes all things to work together for good to those who love God, to those who are called according to *His* purpose" (Rom. 8:28 NASB). And that purpose? That all who believe will be finally conformed to the image of Christ in heaven, in resurrection bodies.

Nothing in all the universe, physical or spiritual, brings God as much glory as this salvation he works through his Son, and God bends all his power toward ensuring it will happen. Every atom and every second is bringing about his ultimate purpose of saving a vast multitude of elect people from every nation on earth.

Amazing Providences in Church History

Throughout history, we have seen God work amazing providences to ensure that aspects of his redemptive plan would take place. He orchestrated a vicious electrical storm to cause Martin Luther to make a terror-filled pledge to forsake his father's plan that he should be a prosperous lawyer and decide instead to become a monk.[6] He orchestrated a war between Charles V of Spain and Francis I of France, at least in part to cause troop movements that blocked the road to Strasbourg, where John Calvin wanted to go for a life of quiet scholarly pursuits.[7] Because of these blocked roads, Calvin diverted to Geneva, where he was met by William Farel, who passionately and effectively convinced him to settle down and minister in that city where he would spend most of the rest of his life.

John Newton was a slave trader, blasphemer, and immoral man. On March 21, 1748, he was on a ship on his way home to England in the North Atlantic. A violent storm rocked the ship, and every hand laid hold of the ropes to try to keep her afloat. As Newton was about to go forward to tend to the sails, the captain stopped him and had him fetch a knife. The sailor who went forward in Newton's place was immediately washed overboard. Newton never forgot that. He survived that storm and began seeking faith in Christ by reading Scripture. He was soundly converted, and every year for fifty years after that, he observed that date with fasting, prayer, and humiliation.[8] His hymn "Amazing Grace" celebrates God's work in his life and is one of the most cherished hymns in church history.

Charles Spurgeon, as a teenager, was engaged in desperate spiritual struggle and sought out someone who could explain to him in simple terms the message of salvation. Later, in his testimony, he recalled the kindness of God in sending a snowstorm that closed the church he was intending to visit, causing him to turn into a Primitive Methodist chapel, a place he would never have attended for any other reason. The blizzard prevented the ordinary preacher from coming, but a lay preacher got up and preached from Isaiah 45: "Look unto me, and be ye saved, all the ends of the earth" (v. 22 KJV). The powerful application made by this bold, uneducated, lower-class man so pierced Spurgeon that he was converted on the spot.[9]

These stories will be multiplied in heaven. God sends forth signal providences in every Christian's life, more than we will ever remember. They remind us that God reigns over everyday life occurrences to save and sanctify souls. So the next time you're stuck in traffic and can't imagine why God would have you blocked from your intended plans, keep these stories in mind.

Providence Is Essential to Christian Contentment

This doctrine of God's meticulous providential rule over the world is vital to Christian contentment. Christian contentment is finding delight in God's wise plan for my life and humbly allowing him to direct me in it. Without providence, it would be impossible to find this contentment "in any and every circumstance." Without the belief that God rules over every atom and every moment, we might think, as unbelievers do, that this or that situation had come to us by "luck" or "karma." We would miss the wise purpose in all of life's events. And it would be impossible for us to maintain a sweet, inward, quiet submission to a set of random events that did not come from God.

five

THE MYSTERIOUS MINDSET
OF CONTENTMENT

Like all aspects of Christian growth, the battle for supernatural contentment is a battle for the mind. Paul says in Romans 12:2 that we are transformed by the renewing of our minds; so it will be as we learn the secret of Christian contentment. Following Jeremiah Burroughs's guidance, here are seven of the key aspects of this mysterious mindset.[1]

Perfectly Satisfied While Totally Dissatisfied

Burroughs shows the marvel of a Christian who has learned the secret of Christian contentment: such a person is perfectly content in the most demeaning and humiliating circumstances that can be found in this world—prison, torture, poverty, public ridicule and censure, chronic pain, even death.[2] But they would be completely discontent if you offered them the entire world instead of heaven. If you give a contented Christian bread and water for dinner and a tattered blanket to sleep under, they can lie down at peace. But they are wary of what the pursuit of ever-increasing wealth and power would do to their souls (Matt. 16:26).

The combination of complete satisfaction *in* the world and complete dissatisfaction *with* the world is a mystery of contentment.

Subtracting Desires Until They Equal God's Providence

There is a heavenly arithmetic to Christian contentment: subtraction and addition.[3]

First, the subtraction. We become content not by adding to our possessions and pleasures, but by *subtracting* from our desires, carving them down until they equal what our loving heavenly Father chooses to provide. Worldly people are restless because they always desire more, more, a little more. Such was the case for the wealthiest man in history, John D. Rockefeller, who relentlessly built an empire that controlled 90 percent of the oil industry in the United States.[4] When asked, "How much is enough?" his famous reply was, "Just a little bit more."[5]

Contented Christians have learned to carve down their desires until they match what God wants for us. Get rid of earthly ambitions that are hurting you. Paul said it is the *love* of money, not money itself, that is the root of all manner of evil (1 Tim. 6:10). So also worldly ambitions for fame, power, fleshly experiences, and glittering possessions drive our hearts inexorably toward deep discontentment.

A famous sculptor once was asked how he could turn a lifeless block of stone into a horse that seemed so vibrantly alive. He answered, "I choose a block of marble, then carve away everything that doesn't look like a horse."[6] In a way, practitioners of Christian contentment are skillful sculptors who learn to sculpt away from their expectations everything that doesn't line up with God's Word and God's providential purposes for their life.

The journey I took as a new Christian with one text of Scripture helps illustrate this mentality. The text is Psalm 37:4: "Delight yourself in the LORD, and he will give you the desires of your heart." When I first read this, it became a treasured verse that I believed to mean, "If I love Jesus, he will give me anything I want." After a while, I grew into a more mature outlook. This verse morphed subtly into this: "Take delight in the Lord, and he will assign me what I should want." Then, finally, it became, "Take delight in Christ, and he will *become* your heart's desire." And he will satisfy it more richly than we can ask or think.

Adding Little by Little the Burden of What You Deserve

The other half of the arithmetic of contentment is addition.

We do not seek so much to rid ourselves of the burdens of our afflictions as to add to our souls a deeper and more truthful appraisal of our sinfulness and what it deserves. There is an inherent humility in Christian contentment and a basic arrogance in discontentment. Jesus likened our forgiveness to a debt of ten thousand talents (Matt. 18:24). Such a figure would have staggered the minds of his hearers, because a talent was seventy-five pounds of gold or silver. The sum of ten thousand talents would be equivalent in the modern world to billions of dollars in debt.

Most of us Christians do not feel the magnitude of that debt. When we first come to Christ, we only begin to see the sin problem. The Holy Spirit will spend the rest of our lives making us increasingly aware not only of the ten thousand talents we owed at conversion, but the ongoing depth of depravity in our present hearts and lifestyles. Every Christian should take Psalm 139 to God in prayer: "Search me, O God, and know my heart! Try me and know my thoughts! And see if there be any grievous way in me, and lead me in the way everlasting!" (vv. 23–24). The Spirit will reveal the hidden pockets of sin in our life, and we will gain a healthy humility before such a holy God.

What follows our discovery of hidden sin is a sense of what that sin truly deserves—the eternal wrath of God in hell. Paradoxically, studying the horrors of hell can be a gateway to a resilient joy "in any and every circumstance." We walk through that gateway when we realize that we deserve to be in hell and instead are here on earth now. There is no condition on earth worse than hell: not suffering the ravages of disease in an ICU, not being incarcerated in a POW camp, not being in a sailboat in the midst of a hurricane, not even grieving at the funeral of a child. And as sinners, we all deserve to be in hell *right now*. But, thanks be to God, Christ drank hell for us on the cross, freeing us from the condemnation the law of God says we deserved (Rom. 3:9–10; 8:1).

These thoughts are humbling, and they give real spiritual teeth to the statement that some Christians make rather glibly when asked, "How are you doing?" In response they say, "Better than I deserve!" And yes, that is true, but how infinitely do we underestimate it.

Embracing the Absolute Necessity of Suffering

A person who has learned the secret of being content in any and every circumstance has learned it by experience through the school of suffering. As we have noted, the apostle Paul's résumé of suffering is the greatest in church history (2 Cor. 11:23–28), and it was the combination of his understanding of doctrine and his experiences of suffering in the world that achieved the learning of this secret.

Suffering is essential to kingdom growth. Jesus taught us this principle plainly: "Truly, truly, I say to you, unless a grain of wheat falls into the earth and dies, it remains alone; but if it dies, it bears much fruit. Whoever loves his life loses it, and whoever hates his life in this world will keep it for eternal life" (John 12:24–25). We must conquer the natural desire for a painless life if we are going to grow in contentment and advance the kingdom of Christ in a hostile world.

Doing the Duty of the Circumstance

Burroughs said every Christian should seek to do "the duty of the circumstance."[7] In other words, what does God want me to do here and now? What is unique about this set of circumstances that enables me to put the glory of Christ and the sweetness of the gospel on display here? How is this set of circumstances a lampstand on which I have been placed that I may glorify God and show to onlookers the sweetness of the gospel of Jesus Christ?

Jesus said, "You are the light of the world. A city set on a hill cannot be hidden. Nor do people light a lamp and put it under a basket, but on a stand, and it gives light to all in the house. In the same way, let your light shine before others, so that they may see your good works and give glory to your Father who is in heaven" (Matt. 5:14–16). Could it be that he has orchestrated this cancer and all its diagnostics and treatments so that I may be a witness to other patients and to the medical community that will surround me during this time?

Conversely, when any success or prosperity comes into our lives, we should not merely bask in the happiness of the moment as any pagan would, but we should see how God wants us to use that prosperity or success to advance the kingdom of Christ. I remember February of 2000, when St. Louis Rams quarterback Kurt Warner won the Super Bowl with a thrilling game-winning pass to Isaac Bruce. With hundreds of millions of people watching, ABC's interviewer on the field, Mike Tirico, asked the hero of the day, "Kurt, first things first, tell me about the final touchdown pass to Isaac!" And with a smile and a strong, clear voice, Warner replied, "Well, first things first, I've got to thank my Lord and Savior up above!" Then he shouted as loud as he could, with no shame at all: "Thank you, Jesus!" He seized the moment for Christ rather than being swept away in the worthless and temporary adulation of a fickle world. He and his wife Brenda then went on to start a Christian charity called the First Things First Foundation.[8]

Every day, Christians should ponder Ephesians 2:10: "We are his workmanship, created in Christ Jesus for good works, which God prepared beforehand, that we should walk in them." God in his wise providence orchestrates specific situations every single day for us Christians, and there are specific good works that he has prepared in advance for us to walk in.

We miss many of those good works by being filled with our own selfish focus, not to mention any feelings of discontent.

Purging Inner Corruptions

We earth-bound, unglorified Christians are deeply divided creatures.

We are "new creations" in Christ (2 Cor. 5:17), yet we are still infected with "sin that dwells within" us (Rom. 7:17), a condition worse than any metastatic cancer.

> The flesh desires what is against the Spirit, and the Spirit desires what is against the flesh; these are opposed to each other, so that you don't do what you want. (Gal. 5:17 CSB)

> So I discover this law: when I want to do what is good, evil is present with me. For in my inner self I delight in God's law, but I see a different law in the parts of my body, waging war against the law of my mind and taking me prisoner to the law of sin in the parts of my body. What a wretched man I am! Who will rescue me from this body of death? (Rom. 7:21–24 CSB)

Our indwelling sin will wage war against contentment every step of the way. And that indwelling sin is far deeper within us than we can possibly imagine. God allowed Satan to hit Job with an avalanche of trials: the death of all his children, the loss of all his wealth, and a severe and painful disease. Initially, Job responded with amazing perspective: "The LORD gave, and the LORD has taken away; blessed be the name of the LORD" (Job 1:21). But as the trial wore on, his inner sins started bubbling to the surface: "God . . . has deprived me of justice" (27:2 CSB).

Our divided hearts are like gold mixed with impurities. In ancient times, goldsmiths would put gold in a crucible and subject it to the refiner's fire—over 1000°F. This would cause the impurities to float to the surface, where they could be skimmed off. The process could be repeated many times. Psalm 12:6 speaks of "silver refined in a furnace on the ground, purified seven times." So it is with the entire sanctification process. And until God purges all sin from within us, discontentment will continue to exert its strong pull on us.

Embracing That Life Is a Mist

The brevity of life is a vital meditation for any who would attain Christian contentment. We are told that our life is a mist, like a morning vapor rising from the bog that the mid-day sun will easily drive away (James 4:14). Moses asked God to "teach us to number our days, that we may get a heart of wisdom" (Ps. 90:12). Time is brief; eternity, endless. James Joyce captured a sense of this in his *Portrait of the Artist as a Young Man*:

> You have often seen the sand on the seashore. How fine are its tiny grains! And how many of those tiny little grains go to make up the small handful which a child grasps in its play. Now imagine a mountain of that sand, a million miles high, reaching from the earth to the farthest heavens, and a million miles broad, extending to remotest space, and a million miles in thickness; and imagine such an enormous mass

of countless particles of sand multiplied as often as there are leaves in the forest, drops of water in the mighty ocean, feathers on birds, scales on fish, hairs on animals, atoms in the vast expanse of the air: and imagine that at the end of every million years a little bird came to that mountain and carried away in its beak a tiny grain of that sand. How many millions upon millions of centuries would pass before that bird had carried away even a square foot of that mountain, how many eons upon eons of ages before it had carried away all? Yet at the end of that immense stretch of time not even one instant of eternity could be said to have ended. At the end of all those billions and trillions of years eternity would have scarcely begun.[9]

This makes me realize that anything I experience here on earth is so fleeting, like a whisper that barely tickles the eardrum and then is gone.

Paul, the one with the overwhelming résumé of suffering, had these two things to say:

For this light momentary affliction is preparing for us an eternal weight of glory beyond all comparison. (2 Cor. 4:17)

For I consider that the sufferings of this present time are not worth comparing with the glory that is to be revealed in us. (Rom. 8:18)

Both of these verses say that the sufferings we go through in this present world are infinitely insignificant compared to the eternity of glory that will follow. The more that we really believe our sufferings don't begin to compare to our future glory, the more content we will be in suffering. In the

2 Corinthians verse, Paul also says the sufferings are preparing us for that glory. We believe that, by suffering well for Christ and his kingdom, we will actually receive a reward that will bring us pleasure for all eternity. As Jesus said to his persecuted followers: "Rejoice and be glad, for your reward is great in heaven, for so they persecuted the prophets who were before you" (Matt. 5:12). The more we sacrificially live for God's glory now, the greater our capacity will be to enjoy that glory in heaven.

The eternal perspective also makes accumulating wealth, power, accolades, or anything for outward show appear so frivolous. Just imagine sharing a room in a nice hotel with a friend on a business trip in Chicago. After checking in and putting his luggage down in your room, he says he has an important errand to run. You go with him and are shocked when he walks into a home-decorating store and begins picking out carpets, drapes, framed pictures, and other accessories. You ask him what in the world he's doing, and he says, "I'm decorating our room! It was too modern for my taste." You look at him like he's crazy. "We're only staying for two nights!" To a certain extent the same is true for us as Christians: we're just passing through. The apostle Peter calls us "aliens and strangers" in this world (1 Pet. 2:11 NASB).

John Wesley captured the fleeting glory of this world with this journal entry:

> I was in the robe-chamber, adjoining to the House of Lords, when the King put on his robes. His brow was much furrowed with age, and quite clouded with care. And is this all the world can give even to a King? All the grandeur it can afford? A blanket of ermine around his shoulders, so heavy

and cumbersome he can scarce move under it! A huge heap of borrowed hair, with a few plates of gold and glittering stones upon his head! Alas, what a bauble is human greatness! And even this will not endure.[10]

This particular king was King George II, ruler of Great Britain, who was at this point at the height of his power. But here was this seventy-two-year-old monarch looking frail, worn, and ugly. Within five years he would be dead, his aorta having ruptured while he sat on the toilet. What an ugly and inglorious way for a king to die!

So why should we care if the world notices or honors us? And why should we get cosmetic surgery or botox treatments to fight off the ravages of old age? Looking at life as a mist, and knowing that the important perspective is the eternal one, will free us from needing to be compensated for our labors for the Lord, or thanked by our spouse, or praised by the church for our years of service. This perspective will serve us well now and help us grow into the stable Christian contentment that Paul knew.

In this chapter, we have walked through some of the mysterious elements of delighting in and humbly following God's wise plan for our lives. No doubt as we live this out, our lives will stand in stark contrast to the world of discontented unbelievers around us daily. And that is a very good thing, for eternal fruit may well come from the conversations that will follow.

six

How Christ Teaches Contentment

The life of Jesus Christ is a massive and perfect diamond of glory, with an infinite number of facets that throw off radiance and dazzle the eyes of his followers for eternity. In this chapter, I want to reveal some particular facets of Christ's glory by how he teaches contentment to Christians.

Every disciple is enrolled in Christ's "school of contentment." The teaching in this school is hardly placid; we don't sit in a comfortable classroom. The author of Hebrews calls Christ the "author and perfecter" of our faith (12:2 NASB). Jesus is the example of contentment, the intrepid pioneer leading the way through enemy territory, and the mighty captain fighting our spiritual enemies and perfecting our contentment in heaven. These lessons come while the pupils are under constant enemy fire.

So, how exactly does Christ teach us contentment?

By His Example

Burroughs taught us that Christian contentment is a "sweet, inward, quiet, gracious frame of spirit, which freely submits to and delights in God's wise and fatherly disposal in every condition."[1] Let's take that definition and apply it to Jesus.

Before he was born, Jesus occupied a throne of glory but did not count equality with God something to be grasped. He emptied himself of the outward display of his glory and made himself as the lowliest slave (Phil. 2:6–7). He entered in the form of a human being, a helpless baby. He was not born into luxury but into staggeringly humble circumstances, wrapped in swaddling clothes and laid in a feeding trough for animals because there was no room in the inn.

As he grew up in the home of Joseph and Mary, Jesus submitted to their authority over him in perfect obedience to the law of Moses (Luke 2:51). He was born under the law and lived every moment of his life under the law, never violating a single detail for an instant (Gal. 4:4). As his public ministry began, he embraced an ever-downward journey of obedience to his Father's will, serving the constant needs of sick, suffering, and dying people, swimming in a sea of misery, drinking in the suffering and taking it into himself, being "a man of sorrows and acquainted with grief" (Isa. 53:3). His obedience led him to be despised and rejected by his own people, condemned by Jews and gentiles alike. He willingly submitted to death, even the most horrific and shameful death imaginable—death on a cross (Phil. 2:8).

This downward journey of suffering is the matrix by which we can see his astonishing example of contentment "in any and every circumstance." Jesus continually displayed peace, such that he could say, "Peace I leave with you; my peace I give to you. Not as the world gives do I give to you. Let not your hearts be troubled, neither let them be afraid" (John 14:27). Despite immense suffering and anguish of soul and body, Jesus displayed the triumph of contentment in his Father's will in Gethsemane, then modeled a stunning display of peace even when on trial, tortured, and executed.

The summit of Christ's example of "freely [submitting] to and [delighting] in God's wise and fatherly disposal" came at the cross. We see the submission perfectly acted out in Gethsemane. There the Father revealed to him in a new and much more powerful way the cup of his wrath that he would pour out on Jesus as our substitute, and Christ recoiled in amazement.[2] Since Jesus had known throughout his ministry that he would die for the sins of the people, this "amazement" could very well have been the Father revealing to Jesus' human understanding just what it would be like to be "made . . . to be sin" for his people (2 Cor. 5:21) and to drink the cup of God's wrath in our place. It was like hell on earth.

And with the revelation of this horror by the Father came the implicit question: "My Son, will you do it?" Jesus' obedient answer, "Not my will, but yours be done," is the pinnacle of a human being freely submitting to the "wise and fatherly disposal" of Almighty God. And the fact that he "delights" in that disposal? Hebrews 12:2 calls us to look to Jesus, "who for the *joy* that was set before him endured the cross, despising the shame." Jesus understood that the will of God meant eternal salvation for a multitude greater than anyone could count from every nation on earth and a perfect display of the glory of God (Rev. 7:9–10). And that brought Christ delight and contentment, despite the infinite cost to himself. There is no higher example in human history of perfect contentment.

And in the events that followed Gethsemane, we see Jesus living out this contentment with amazing power. The Gospel accounts set Jesus up in striking contrast to everyone around him. He was content to do the will of his Father, even to the point of dying on the cross, in a stunning display of peace. He stood in the eye of a hurricane as everyone around him was ripped from the ground and thrown into the air. His submission to the Father was in stark contrast to others such as Judas, the Jewish authorities, Pontius Pilate, the soldiers who flogged him, the citizens of Jerusalem who mocked him, and even his scattering disciples. He taught us how to suffer intensely under the hand of God. And by his wounds as well as his example we are healed from all sin, including discontentment (Isa. 53:5). However, we should not minimize how much this cost him, and how immeasurable were his sufferings for us. He cried out, "My God, my God, why have you forsaken me?" His supernatural peace can be seen more in his words and actions toward others: his words during his trials and his beatings, his words to the women of Jerusalem. Even on the cross, his statements concerning the soldiers who crucified him ("Father, forgive them"), his mother and John, and the thief on the cross ("Today, you will be with me in Paradise") show an other-centeredness and peace that is amazing.

By His God-Centeredness

Throughout his entire life, Jesus perfectly displayed this Father-centered focus:

My food is to do the will of him who sent me and to accomplish his work. (John 4:34)

I have come down from heaven, not to do my own will but the will of him who sent me. (John 6:38)

I do nothing on my own authority, but speak just as the Father taught me. . . . He has not left me alone, for I always do the things that are pleasing to him. (John 8:28–29)

I have not spoken on my own authority, but the Father who sent me has himself given me a commandment—what to say and what to speak. And I know that his commandment is eternal life. What I say, therefore, I say as the Father has told me. (John 12:49–50)

Jesus did nothing, spoke no words, went nowhere, ate no food, and drank no drink except according to the detailed plan of his Father. The detailed plan and will of his Father hemmed in his life every single day that he lived. In his temptation in the desert, Satan constantly tried to separate Jesus from his Father. But Jesus would not turn the stones into bread because he lived and ate bread only at the word of his Father. He would not eat again until the Father told him to eat. He would not throw himself from the pinnacle of the temple, expecting the Father to dispatch angels to save him, because his Father had not told him to do that, and that would have been to put his Father to the test. Jesus would not bow down and worship Satan, though he could have gained the whole world by so doing, because Jesus worshiped the Lord his God and served him only (Matt. 4:1–11). Jesus' absolute focus on the glory of the Father was the essence of his sinlessness. To use an analogy from Burroughs, tempting a content man is like shooting flaming arrows at an iron wall. The arrows that would bring discontent would not pierce through his armor.[3]

For our own contentment, we must become more and more God-centered, focused on the plans and glory of the Father. Much of our discontent comes from our selfishness in pursuing our own agendas, seeking our own glory, feeding our own lusts. We were created to be God-centered servants of his will, moment by moment.

By His Atonement

It is impossible to measure all the blessings that have been purchased by Christ's blood shed on the cross. By his blood, all our sins are forgiven—past, present, and future (Eph. 1:7). By his blood, the price has been paid for our adoption as sons and daughters of God (Gal. 4:5). By his blood, we have been qualified to share in an infinitely valuable inheritance with all the saints in perfect light (Col. 1:12).

So how do we allow Satan to deceive us into thinking that our present earthly circumstances are equivalent to even a millionth of a part of even one of these gifts of grace? How can we look upon these blessings and say, "Yes, all these things are true, but still . . . look at how much I am suffering! Look at what I have recently lost! I am and should be bitterly discontent!" We ought to stand on the permanent blessings of the atonement and by Christ's Spirit drive out every moment of discontent from our lives, no matter how fierce the battle for contentment may be!

We must see that Christ's death was the most unexpected means of salvation for the people of God. Unexpected and unforeseen. Each of Christ's disciples was stunned when he died and could not comprehend how his death was part of God's eternal plan. Peter tried to talk Jesus out of it by his rebukes (Matt. 16:22) and tried to rescue Jesus from it by his dagger (26:51). The two disciples on the road to Emmaus were depressed and acted as if Jesus' death disqualified him from being the one who would redeem Israel (Luke 24:21).

Though the church would eventually come to understand the cross, their initial instincts went badly astray, and their tendency was to question God most severely. But God's eternal plans will be costly to us and will violate our wisdom and desires. When we are in the midst of those painful trials, we should remember the lessons of the cross and be content, though our wisdom and desires scream the opposite.

By His Resurrection

If Christ ministers contentment by his death, then how much more does he minister contentment by his resurrection?

If a dead Jesus on the cross is an unending supply of peace and joy in any and every circumstance, how much more does a living Christ in heaven have power to minister contentment to his embattled church?

By Christ's resurrection, we know that death has been defeated—we will look in triumph over death and say, "O death, where is your victory? O death, where is your sting?" (1 Cor. 15:55). Christ's resurrection gives us full confidence that all of our labors and sufferings for Christ in this life are not in vain, but lead to a glorious end (v. 58). By his resurrection, we have been made spiritually alive, even though we were once dead in our transgressions and sins (Eph. 2:1–5). By his Spirit, we are united with him in resurrection power and are enabled to walk in newness of life (Rom. 6:4).

The empty tomb gives us immeasurable power for contentment in any and every circumstance. It gives us hope when we face bodily suffering and pain, even death. We know that our resurrection bodies will be glorious, powerful, incorruptible, incapable of ever dying again (1 Cor. 15:42–43; Rev. 21:4). That hope is intimately connected with contentment.

So when we are facing adverse circumstances as Christians, we can drive away discontent by the truth of Christ's resurrection. We can say to the temptation, "It is true that I am suffering and in great pain. It is true that my earthly condition is the worst I have ever experienced. But this one thing I know: Christ is risen and he has therefore defeated death. And he did not defeat death for himself; he defeated it for me. Someday, I will emerge from my tomb in a resurrection body that will shine like the sun in the kingdom of my Father!"

By Winning for Us Access to God

Christ has won for us the continual access to the Father that is essential to maintaining contentment in any and every circumstance. Apart from that access in prayer, we would certainly fall into bitter discontentment, for the world, the flesh, and the devil are foes far too great for us. But by prayer, we can unleash the power of God in our hearts and into our circumstances that will enable us to stand in the day of testing.

In 2001, I had the opportunity to visit the Forbidden City in Beijing. It is a vast complex of almost eight hundred wooden buildings that served for over five centuries as the imperial palace for the ruling emperors of the Ming and Qing dynasties. Built by one hundred thousand skilled craftsmen and over a million laborers, its sole purpose was to provide a secluded space where the emperor of China would be free from interacting with the common people. It was called the Forbidden City because only by the permission of the emperor could anyone either enter or leave. Within the vast complex, there is a series of walls, courtyards, and gates barring access to the emperor. The Gate of Supreme Harmony is the final gate before the imperial throne, and no commoner was able to get that far. The Imperial Court consisted of one hundred thousand selected people who served as the emperor's officials, but even they rarely got to glimpse the emperor. Whenever the emperor wanted to review his Imperial Court, he would summon them to the courtyard called the Hall of Supreme Harmony. An official would call out the emperor's arrival, and all the court officials would fall to their knees and kowtow (touch their foreheads to the floor) before him nine times. This was a symbol of their complete obedience to him as the Son of Heaven, the emperor of China.[4]

As I walked in the midst of these ancient walls and the courtyards leading to courtyards leading to more courtyards, I couldn't help but ponder the access we all have to the true Emperor of the Universe, Almighty God, through the true Son of Heaven, the Lord Jesus Christ. The Old Testament worship commanded by the law of Moses focused on a place where all the Jews would bring their animal sacrifices. For many centuries, this place was a moveable tent called the tabernacle. Then in the days of King Solomon, a temple was built. Both places taught the same lesson from Almighty God: "This far you may come, and no farther." Inside both the tabernacle and the temple was a curtain barring even the priests from entering into the Most Holy Place, where God was symbolically ruling. This curtain represented the old covenant's overpowering message of exclusion for sinners.

At the moment of Christ's death, the curtain in the temple was torn in two from top to bottom (Matt. 27:51). God was showing by this that Christ's atoning death had forever removed this barrier; the way into his holy presence was now opened: "Therefore, brothers, since we have confidence to enter the holy places by the blood of Jesus, by the new and living way that he opened for us through the curtain, that is, through his flesh, and since we have a great priest over the house of God, let us draw near with a true heart in full assurance of faith, with our hearts sprinkled clean from an evil conscience and our bodies washed with pure water" (Heb. 10:19–22).

This "new and living way" means access for sinners into the very presence of God. Therefore, we are actually commanded—not merely encouraged or welcomed—to draw near to God: "Let us then with confidence draw near to the throne of grace, that we may receive mercy and find grace to help in time of need" (Heb. 4:16). Whenever we are in a battle with discontentment, it is a "time of need." We cannot fight alone; we must draw near to the throne of grace and receive mercy and find grace. If we don't, we will most certainly succumb to the power of the temptation to murmur against God. But by prayer alone we will gain access to the limitless strength needed to stand up in the day of temptation.

By His Presence

No doubt the trials we face are exceptionally severe and press us to the limits of our endurance. There are many times in which we feel we cannot take much more of the pressure. But the greatest comfort to us is this one timeless assertion: "I will never leave you nor forsake you" (Heb. 13:5). To have Jesus stand with us, ministering his comfort as we endure trials too difficult to face alone, is unspeakably precious. It is essential to contentment.

The apostle Paul received this incredible ministry from Christ at several key moments in his life of suffering for the gospel. The most powerful of these moments occurred when Paul was on trial for his life before Caesar (Nero): "At my first defense no one came to stand by me, but all deserted me. May it not be charged against them! *But the Lord stood by me and strengthened me*, so that through me the message might be fully proclaimed and all the Gentiles might hear it. So I was rescued from the lion's mouth" (2 Tim. 4:16–17). It is hard to draw out sufficiently the emotional poignancy of these words.

Imagine standing before a maniacal tyrant like Nero with the full gospel message: "Repent of your sins and trust in Christ for your salvation!" Imagine the terror that could strike any normal man who was on trial for his life. How could anyone have inner peace and joy at such a time? And imagine having not a single friendly face in the throne room of the Roman emperor—only hostile opposition. All of

Paul's friends had deserted him, possibly to save their own lives. The "lion," Satan, was prowling around seeking to prevent him from finishing his race and fulfilling his ministry of fully preaching the gospel to the king of the gentiles. Yet suddenly Paul was overwhelmed by a sense of Christ's presence so real and palpable that a surge of power and boldness came upon him. The Lord stood at Paul's side! The Lord gave Paul strength! And the message was fully proclaimed to Caesar and to all his officials.

Christ has stood at the side of believers time and time again throughout the history of the church, especially when Christians are being persecuted for their faith. Recently I was reading an amazing story of twenty-three Korean missionaries who had been held hostage by the Taliban in Afghanistan in July of 2007. These missionaries all knew that martyrdom was a distinct possibility. But on the last day of their imprisonment together, they made a solemn pact to surrender their mortal lives willingly to God. They even argued about which of them would get to die first! One of them had smuggled a Bible into the cell, and they ripped it into twenty-three portions so each of them could have some Scripture to get them through. Eventually two of them were martyred, but the others were released. They held a reunion of sorts, and all of them testified the same thing: they had had such an overwhelming sense of the presence of Christ through the Holy Spirit that they actually wished they were still in the cell.[5]

We are not likely to face trials of this magnitude. But we will walk through things that will challenge our souls. Jesus promises us: "Fear not, for I have redeemed you; I have called you by name, you are mine. When you pass through the waters, I will be with you; and through the rivers, they shall not overwhelm you; when you walk through fire you shall not be burned, and the flame shall not consume you" (Isa. 43:1–2).

By His Demands

One of the most comforting passages in the Bible contains a comprehensive demand to submit to Christ's kingly authority: "Come to me, all who labor and are heavy laden, and I will give you rest. Take my yoke upon you, and learn from me, for I am gentle and lowly in heart, and you will find rest for your souls. For my yoke is easy, and my burden is light" (Matt. 11:28–30). This is indeed a sweet and comforting passage, but it is easy for us to miss the significance of the word "yoke." In the Old Testament, a yoke either referred to a literal piece of wood put across the necks of beasts of burden to control them and make them work for the farmer or was used metaphorically to represent authority, often tyrannical kingly authority. God says he rescued Israel from the yoke of slavery under the Egyptians (Lev. 26:13). The image of a yoke of iron is the very thing the prophet Jeremiah used to predict the exile to Babylon under the dominion of a tyrant (Jer. 28–30). On the other hand, the prophet Isaiah speaks of a child who would be born, called "Wonderful Counselor, Mighty God, Everlasting Father, Prince of Peace," on whose shoulders the government will rest. It is said of this amazing ruler that he will shatter the yoke that burdens his people and the rod across their shoulders (Isa. 9:4, 6–7). This is a clear picture of the salvation that Christ comes to bring. We were oppressed and helpless (Matt. 9:36), and Jesus came to rescue us from the yoke of slavery to Satan and to sin.

But it is essential that we realize God does not free us from having any yoke at all. We must submit to *his* kingly yoke; we must bow our stiff necks and yield full obedience to him as our king. This is the essence of entering the kingdom of God—to cease our rebellion against his rule in our lives. God created us to be servants, not autonomous rulers of our own little kingdoms. Satan deceived us into thinking we could rule ourselves and set up our own worlds as we saw fit. No one, not even God, need tell us what to do. This is impossible. For we are in God's universe; he is the creator, king, and ruler of all things. When Christ comes to save us, the essence of that salvation is that we cease rebelling against his good and loving laws.

The good news of the gospel for the rest of our lives is that Christ's yoke is easy and his burden is light—not like the previous master we were serving. Satan hates us and wants to steal, kill, and destroy (John 10:10). God teaches a contentment that rests peacefully under Christ's light yoke.

By Teaching Us the Immeasurable Worth of the Kingdom of Heaven

Jesus told a parable to teach us how much more valuable the kingdom of heaven is than everything we possess: "The kingdom of heaven is like treasure hidden in a field, which a man found and covered up. Then in his joy he goes and sells all that he has and buys that field" (Matt. 13:44).

One may well imagine the man digging feverishly in that field after his shovel hit a metallic object. He digs around the object for an hour, lifts it out, pries off the ancient lock, and uses all his might to lift the iron-bound lid from the chest.

Rummaging through the treasure, hearing the tinkle of countless gold and silver coins, seeing the sparkle of priceless gems as he lifts them up one after the other in the noonday sun— these moments he will never forget for the rest of his life. What he found not only filled him with joy but it immediately made obvious his decision to hide the treasure carefully back in the field, sell all his worldly possessions, and buy that field.

Without taking the time to investigate what was in the chest, the man would be a foolish gambler. Suppose he never opened the box to appraise its contents but on wild speculation sold everything to buy that field. The box might be empty or might contain a dead animal; it could be filled with worthless papers. The parable only makes sense if the Lord expects us to take a faith-based inventory of the treasures of salvation. What do these include? Full forgiveness of all our sins, imputation of Christ's perfect righteousness, adoption into the family of God, the indwelling Holy Spirit, a guaranteed inheritance in heaven, fellowship with brothers and sisters from every nation on earth, a lifetime of worthwhile works to do for his glory, a future resurrection body, and everlasting spiritual treasures unto infinity! How vast and great and immeasurable are the mercies of God! The more we take inventory of this wealth, the more we will realize that Christ *is* the sum of all these treasures, for in him are hidden all the treasures of God (Col. 2:3). And the more content we will become.

By Teaching Us How to Defeat Our Fear and Anxiety

Fear and anxiety are two of the greatest contentment thieves we will ever face. Fear is a normal response to a clear and present danger. Anxiety is the result of an active imagination of possible dangers that may come at us in the future. Christ assaulted both of these by the weapon of faith. When Jesus was asleep in the back of the boat on the Sea of Galilee in the midst of a savage storm, his disciples were terrified and woke him, saying, "Teacher, do you not care that we are perishing?" (Mark 4:38). Their fears were, it seems, well grounded. They saw the water filling the boat; they'd been in many storms on that lake before and could see that their lives were in immediate peril. Jesus was asleep on a cushion, seemingly unconcerned about anything going on at all.

But when Jesus was aroused by their terrorized calls, he rebuked the wind and waves, saying, "Peace! Be still!" Then he rebuked their fear: "Why are you so afraid? Have you still no faith?" (Mark 4:39). So while fear would indeed have been a natural reaction to the clear and present danger (as evidenced by increased heart rate, shortness of breath, adrenaline rushing through the blood stream, frenzied activity, screams), Jesus wanted these men to live supernaturally by faith. Faith should have told them that God did not send his only begotten Son into the world to die in a tragic boating accident! Faith and fear are often polar opposites in the Bible. Faith drives out fear and thus gives a stable platform for supernatural displays of peace known as Christian contentment.

In the same way, Jesus destroys anxiety by faith. An extended portion of the Sermon on the Mount is devoted to his carefully reasoned attack on anxiety. Matthew 6:25–34 is a step-by-step guidebook on what to do when we feel anxious. It is a very reasonable approach, a logic based on faith. Since there is an omnipotent God who rules heaven and earth, and since he knows very well that you need food and clothing, and since God has such an amazing track record of feeding literally billions of living creatures all over the world every single day, and since God carefully clothes wildflowers with wondrous apparel, why should you use your imagination to think of worst-case scenarios that rob you of Christian contentment? Your days were all ordained before one of them came to be, so worrying will not add one second to your lifespan. You are sons and daughters of the living God; you should be living a supernatural life free from the heart-consuming cares that drive the pagans. Instead, you should be seeking first God's kingdom and his righteousness. That should dominate your thoughts, captivate your heart, and govern your activities for the rest of your days. And if you do seek God and his kingdom above all things, you will be consistently content in his sovereign provision for your lesser needs.

There is no greater example and instructor of contentment than Jesus Christ. In him alone can we find a consistent delight in God's wise plan for our lives and humbly follow that plan day after day.

PART 3

THE VALUE
of CONTENTMENT

seven

THE EXCELLENCE OF CHRISTIAN CONTENTMENT

As I look over the books that have most captivated my attention over the past five years, the common thread among them is their accounts of human excellence: George Washington's leadership in rescuing the American Revolution by his bold crossing of the frozen Delaware River in 1776; Orville and Wilbur Wright's persistence and genius in conquering the air; Lewis and Clark's courage in exploring the American West; Albert Einstein's brilliance in discovering relativity while working as a clerk in the Swiss patent office; Andrew Carnegie's perseverance in rising from immigrant poverty to becoming the wealthiest man in the world. These accounts celebrate what is most excellent in the human character. But they all fall short of the excellence of Christian contentment.

In this chapter, I want to captivate your heart with various aspects of the moral excellence of Christian contentment. The more we prize contentment as a rare jewel of inestimable worth, the more we will pursue it and sacrifice in order to attain it, and the more vigorously we will fight every day to protect it from Satan's attacks.

The Most Excellent Worship

Christian contentment enables us to worship God excellently, in a way far purer and more glorious than any other form, better than hearing a sermon or attending corporate worship without contentment. Above all else, we were created to worship God, to glorify him for his majestic person and his amazing achievements. Isaiah 43:6–7 makes it plain that God created us and redeemed us for his glory. So also Ephesians 1:5–6 says God saves us "to the praise of his glorious grace." The most excellent praise we ever give is independent of his material gifts to us; he does not hire us to praise him as though we were the professional mourners Jesus expelled from Jairus's house (Mark 5:40) or, like a harlot, paid to act as a loving wife when all she really cares about is the silver coin. This is the very thing that Satan accused Job of before God's throne: "Does Job fear God for nothing? Haven't you placed a hedge around him, his household, and everything he owns? You have blessed the work of his hands, and his possessions have increased in the land. But stretch out your hand and strike everything he owns, and he will surely curse you to your face" (Job 1:9–11 CSB). "Does Job fear God for nothing?" really means "Don't you actually pay Job to worship you?" The greatest worship Job ever gave God was when, after his children had all died in a single day and all his possessions had been stolen from him, he fell down and worshiped God: "The LORD gave,

100

and the LORD has taken away; blessed be the name of the LORD" (v. 21).

Burroughs gave a remarkable insight concerning the submission of Christian contentment and how it glorifies God: "In active obedience, we worship God by doing what pleases God, but by passive obedience we worship God by being pleased with what God does."[1] Wow, is that powerful! Pray that to God daily! "O heavenly Father, may everything I do today be an aroma pleasing to you because it is done in faith-filled obedience to your laws. And O heavenly Father, may everything you providentially choose to bring into my life be pleasing to me, because I know you are working out a glorious plan for me and for the whole world!" That is the most excellent worship we will ever give.

Most Filled with All Christian Graces

Burroughs speaks of the "exercise of grace." By this he means the Holy Spirit greatly strengthens Christian graces (virtues) by contentment. The foremost of these graces are the fruit of the Spirit: love, joy, peace, patience, kindness, goodness, faithfulness, gentleness, and self-control (Gal. 5:22–23). One could argue that each of these is an essential ingredient in Christian contentment. Beyond these are such graces as humility, thankfulness, wisdom, stability, and others.

Like muscles or talents, all these graces need exercise in order to get stronger. Recently, my son, Calvin, severely sprained his ankle in a basketball game. In order to be fully healed and ready to rejoin his team, he had to undergo some painful physical therapy. The therapist was not a malicious torturer, a descendant of those who carried out the Spanish

Inquisition. But he had some very creative ways to hurt my son! He had him on various machines that leaned his ankle this way and that, stretching the ligaments, strengthening them by painful exercise. So it is with each of these Christian graces. God orchestrates daily trials to strengthen them all in our souls.

Most Ready to Receive Grace

"God opposes the proud, but gives grace to the humble" (1 Pet. 5:5). Our salvation comes in stages, including the internal journey of sanctification.[2] For growth in Christlikeness, we need more grace—continually more grace. God gives that grace to the humble child of God, who is quiet under his sovereign hand. That is contentment. But God withholds his grace from the proud, and discontentment is a proud state of soul. So Peter continues, "Humble yourselves, therefore, under the mighty hand of God so that at the proper time he may exalt you" (v. 6). The exaltation of full Christian maturity comes after a lifetime of quiet humility under the "wise and fatherly disposal" of God.

Burroughs uses a marvelous analogy of a vessel into which you desire to pour a liquid. If the vessel is shaking all around, you will not even try to pour into it. I recently saw a humorous video of a man using a jackhammer-like rammer. While he is working, his whole body vibrates with the power of this tool as he flattens the ground. Someone hands him a bottled drink. As he tries to drink it, he spills the contents all over his face, hair, shirt, everything!

So it is with us. When God wants to pour his grace into us, he needs us still, quiet, like a steady vessel.

Most Prepared to Serve

Christian contentment also prepares us to serve God. A discontent servant has ceased to obey the master and is actually rebelling against the commands he is giving. God does not need us to serve him. "Nor is he served by human hands, as though he needed anything, since he himself gives to all mankind life and breath and everything" (Acts 17:25). He will put us on a shelf, temporarily disqualifying us from serving him, if we are discontent. "If I speak in the tongues of men and of angels, if I possess all wisdom, if I give all I possess to the poor, but am discontent, angry, frustrated, impatient, grumbling, God will not use me!" (see 1 Cor. 13:1–3). Conversely, a content man or woman is a most excellent servant.

Earlier, we discussed Ephesians 2:10: "For we are his workmanship, created in Christ Jesus for good works, which God prepared beforehand, that we should walk in them." Every single day, God has sovereignly gone ahead of us in his providence and has orchestrated a specific set of complex circumstances in which you are to do good works to build his kingdom. You cannot understand fully how your trip to the supermarket to buy food for the men's prayer breakfast will build his kingdom, but you are happy to serve. And who knows whether the checkout clerk might be open to an invitation to church? Similarly, you cannot understand fully how God has planned out your time in the waiting room of the oncologist as you wait to hear the outcome of your test for cancer, but you are alert to another person in the same waiting room who may not know the Savior. Content people are ready to serve their loving Father at every moment.

Most Difficult to Tempt

We are surrounded at every moment by invisible spiritual enemies in the heavenly realms. Satan and his demons are ready to shoot the flaming arrows of temptation into us, seeking to destroy our lives and our ministries (Eph. 6:10–13, 16). As we already saw, Burroughs says temptations will no more prevail over a contented man than a flaming arrow fired against a metal wall.[3] Conversely, a discontent person is like a bundle of oil-soaked straw, waiting for a single arrow of temptation to ignite it into a raging bonfire of evil desires. Discontentment is a wandering, restless, unstable mindset, very much like the devil in his roaming to and fro over the earth (Job 1:7; 2:2), or like the demons relentlessly seeking a resting place (Matt. 12:43). When David was aimlessly walking out on his rooftop rather than leading his army out in the field, he was ready to be ignited by a single flaming arrow of temptation. All it took was seeing a beautiful woman bathing, and his world changed forever (2 Sam. 11:2).

Content people are quiet under God's hand, completely satisfied with the simple blessings God has chosen for them. They are not covetous, so they cannot be tempted with money or possessions. They are not selfishly ambitious, so they cannot be tempted with worldly power. They are not arrogantly ungracious, so they cannot be tempted with bitter revenge. They have allowed the Holy Spirit to work on their souls, so they expect little in this world; instead, they live for the will of their Father and store up treasure in the next world. They are very hard to tempt.

When, by his writings and reformation of Geneva, John Calvin rose to be a mighty threat to the corrupt medieval

Roman Catholic Church, they sought to tempt him with money or to lodge a false accusation against him concerning the lavish habits he was suspected of having. They did not realize what a simple life Calvin habitually lived. Humility and self-denial were his daily disciplines. He lived modestly, in a small, borrowed apartment, with only the most rudimentary furnishings. He persistently refused salary increases. His writings showed a heart overwhelmed with God's grace in saving such a sinner as he. When he died, by his will he was buried at night in an unmarked tomb, so that his monument might not become a shrine for idolatrous pilgrims to venerate. Calvin lived out Paul's example: "If we have food and clothing, with these we will be content" (1 Tim. 6:8).

Most Comforted by Things Not Seen

Parlor magicians hired to entertain children at birthday parties frequently begin tricks with a display of an empty hand, offering clear proof that there is nothing up their sleeve, nothing in the shiny top hat they are about to set on the table in full view of the fascinated children. Then suddenly— *presto!*—a rabbit is pulled up by the ears, a dove with fluttering wings emerges, a shiny silver dollar flips into view. Something created out of nothing! We adults know that these are just parlor tricks, sleights of hand, practiced technique.

The real wonder is created every day by people who have learned the secret of Christian contentment, who can draw comfort from things they do not even possess. They value something of eternal worth created out of nothing in this present world. Content people draw their true comfort from a heavenly inheritance they do not yet possess. They live on promises of an eternal city and world that is their true treasure (Heb. 11:16). Whether they are wealthy or poor in this life is immaterial; they know this full well. All of it is as temporary as a morning mist (James 4:14). They have set their hearts on Christ, who will someday appear in glory. They have set their minds on heavenly, not earthly things (Col. 3:1–3). And their true inheritance is something they most definitely do not yet have: "Now in this hope we were saved, but hope that is seen is not hope, because who hopes for what he sees [that is, already possesses]? Now if we hope for what we do not see [that is, already possess], we eagerly wait for it with patience" (Rom. 8:24–25 CSB).

Content people can even rest patiently under God's wise and fatherly hand when they ask for things in prayer and God says no. Just learning to trust a God who gives and takes away, who grants some blessings and refuses others, demonstrates an amazing level of spiritual maturity. I do not doubt that God saying no to a blessing we seek in prayer is a strong test to our souls. Paul sought God earnestly, asking for the thorn in the flesh to be removed. Certainly it was a "messenger of Satan" (2 Cor. 12:7), but it was also a messenger from God, to keep him from being conceited and teach him that God's grace is sufficient for him, that God's strength is made perfect in weakness (vv. 7, 9). God said no to Paul, but he said an even better yes.

Most Radiant in Hope

There is a powerful connection between hope and Christian contentment. In this wonderful state of contentment, we are most perfectly displaying the Christian virtue of hope. Hope is a strong and settled assurance that the future is bright based on the promises of God. We don't need any earthly proof—no earthly tokens, no earthly blessings—for hope. Hope has to do with things we do not see, things we do not yet possess. Hope shines most brightly when in a severe and present darkness. This is the very thing the unconverted onlookers do not have. They are "without hope and without God in the world" (Eph. 2:12 CSB). Hope is like a buoyant cork that refuses to stay submerged no matter how many times someone shoves it beneath the surface.

It was by a persistent hope that William Wilberforce was able to lead a twenty-seven-year fight against slavery in England, in spite of one setback after another. One of his greatest personal traits during that arduous journey was a personal buoyancy that was astonishing to his enemies: "It is necessary to watch him as he is blessed with a very sufficient quantity of that enthusiastic spirit, which is so far from yielding that it grows more vigorous with blows."[4] Wilberforce was like a buoyant cork that enemies could not keep down. Contentment keeps you in the fight to the end.

In this chapter, we have seen just how delightful is our delight in and submission to God's wise plan for our lives. This delight is a powerful motivator to spur us on to growth in this vital area.

eight

THE EVILS AND EXCUSES OF A COMPLAINING HEART

As we just saw, Christian contentment is a most excellent state of being. On the contrary, habitual complaining—murmuring, as Burroughs calls it—is a most repulsive state of being. It is beneath the dignity of any Christian. Chapters 7 and 8 together show the attraction of Christian contentment and the repulsion that the rebellion of complaining can produce in a lifetime. Contentment is a force on your soul pulling you upward toward Christlikeness. Esteem contentment highly; hate complaining passionately.

All my life I have been fascinated with magnets. From the first time I saw a paper clip wiggle and twitch, then start to slide across a countertop, accelerating until it smashed into the magnet and stuck to it, I have struggled to understand the invisible force that was at work. The first magnets I studied in elementary school were bar magnets, with *N* for the north pole and *S* for the south pole stamped in the metal. Like all science students, I learned that the invisible force of magnetism is either attraction or repulsion. Opposite poles attract each other, same poles repel. Attraction and repulsion.

So it is with Christian growth. The beginning of the Christian life—conversion—always involves a combination of attraction and repulsion: attracted to Christ, repelled from Satan; attracted to heaven, repelled from hell; attracted to holiness, repelled from sin. God wants us to both flee the wrath to come (Matt. 3:7) and seek the things that are above (Col. 3:1). Attraction and repulsion led to our conversion, and the Holy Spirit uses the same principle to drive us toward Christlikeness every day.

For the rest of your life, God desires for you to be *both* attracted to Christian contentment *and* repulsed from worldly discontentment. This chapter will now fill out the negative, repulsive aspect. Burroughs's goal was very plain in this regard: he wanted his readers to *hate* the wicked habit of complaining against God during afflictions, to see how vile and corrupt a thing it is, but even more than that, he wanted his readers to be honest about how often they have yielded to this sin of murmuring and rebelling against God in the past. Burroughs wanted them to see how many tiny irritations in life have caused them to mumble complaints and how many larger afflictions have led them into deep and foul accusations against the goodness of God. He wanted them to know how consistently negative and bitter they have been toward the trials God has chosen to bring to them and how anxious they have been about further such trials. As Burroughs said, "There is more evil [in the habit of murmuring] than you are aware of."[1]

Think of your normal daily habits. What are you like if you discover you are out of coffee? If you get in your car and it doesn't start or there is something wrong with the engine? If you get a bill you didn't expect? If another driver gives you a rude or angry gesture? If you have chronic irritation with an itchy rash that defies the medication the dermatologist prescribed? If your boss never seems to notice the good work you do or you get passed over for a promotion in your department and it goes to someone you consider inferior to you? And how much worse are your thoughts and words should any severe trial come into your life, like the death of a family member or the loss of your home to a natural disaster?

Do we really have any conception of how many complaints we've uttered in the last year? What would our spouse or our kids or parents say about us, if they had to tell the truth? Do our friends and family members see us as characterized by consistent Christian contentment? Or does God have to do a significant work in our heart and habits to cause us to forsake complaining and murmuring against God in both small and large trials?

In the last chapter, we saw the moral excellence of Christian contentment. Now, we need to take a tour of the dark side. We will discuss first the evils of a murmuring heart. Then we will walk through a few representative excuses people make.

The Evils of Complaining

Complaining Is the Opposite of Praise and Worship

As we began the last chapter with the assertion that we were originally created by God and then redeemed by Christ for the praise and glory of God, we must begin this section by seeing how complaining is the exact opposite of that. Peter says that "you are a chosen race, a royal priesthood, a holy nation, a people for his own possession, that you may proclaim the excellencies of him who called you out of darkness into his marvelous light" (1 Pet. 2:9). God did this amazing work of saving us by the blood of his precious Son so that our mouths might be filled continually with praise. And yet, instead of praising him, we must admit that we have consistently chosen to complain. God gave us a mind and the power of speech, and we are using them to speak against him, to murmur against what he has chosen to bring into our lives, whether great or small affliction. The same mouth that was singing God's praises in church yesterday is now speaking harsh words of complaint about some annoyance in a mall parking lot or some lower back pain. "From the same mouth come blessing and cursing. My brothers, these things ought not to be so" (James 3:10).

Complaining Reveals Much Corruption in the Soul

All of us underestimate how much evil complaining reveals in our hearts. We have spent much of our lives complaining about our surroundings—too hot, too cold, too loud, too soft, too spicy, too bland. We don't think it matters if we voice our frustrations on a regular basis. But actually Scripture teaches the truth: complaining reveals much corruption in the soul.

Burroughs put it this way: "As contentment [reveals] much grace in the soul, strong grace, beautiful grace, so murmuring [reveals] much corruption, strong corruption, vile corruptions in your heart."[2] This extends to both extremes of the scale of affliction. If little things cause such irritation of spirit, how weak must I be? And even if the affliction is great, the toxic effects of murmuring against God are far more damaging to your soul. Burroughs said, "O that we could but convince men and women that a murmuring spirit is a greater evil than any affliction, whatever the affliction!"[3]

There really is no such thing as a small complaint. Think of it as a bleeding wound that drains off your spiritual vitality. You were Spirit-filled after your quiet time, then one thing irks you and you begin complaining, and the Spirit-filled demeanor is gone. Imagine you are a soldier in World War I. You go over the top of the trench with your unit, charge through no-man's-land, cower under multiple artillery blasts, duck machine-gun bullets, then scamper back to the relative safety of your trench. You are breathing hard but thankful to still be alive. Your buddy looks down at your pants and sees a dark and spreading stain. "You're hit!" he yells. You look down and see it. You can't shrug it off; if it is large enough, that opening in your skin could result in you bleeding out, or perhaps in a deadly infection. This is how you must see complaining—as a bleeding wound in your soul, through which the power of the Spirit drains out of you until you repent of it.

Complaining Is the Mark of an Ungodly Generation

One of the greatest sins God charges against the human race is ingratitude: "For although they knew God, they did not honor him as God *or give thanks* to him, but they became futile in their thinking, and their foolish hearts were darkened" (Rom. 1:21). Every single day, God pours out his rich blessings, like sunshine and rain (Matt. 5:45), on a population of people who never give him thanks or praise. Quite the contrary, they grumble against him continually. Jude says that these are the ungodly who are going to be judged by the Lord when he comes: "These are grumblers, malcontents, following their own sinful desires" (Jude 16). Since this is who God singles out and calls "ungodly," why would any Christian want to be like them in grumbling and being malcontent?

Burroughs drives this point home with powerful conviction. He says that his readers may fancy themselves much better than other ungodly people because they don't get drunk or use foul language as do the unconverted. But God looks at us as every bit as ungodly if we join them in murmuring against him.

Complaining Is Considered Rebellion

The definition of Christian contentment settles this clearly: it is a frame of spirit that *freely submits* to God. To be discontent is to fail to submit, and that is nothing less than rebellion. Israel's experience in the desert makes this even more plain. The people of Israel were continually grumbling and complaining against Moses and against God. Right before the Red Sea crossing, when the people saw Pharaoh's army, they said, "Is it because there are no graves in Egypt that you have taken us away to die in the wilderness?" (Exod. 14:11). After the crossing of the Red Sea—the most visually spectacular miracle God ever did—the people immediately started complaining about there being no water to drink. The place was called Massah and Meribah (meaning "quarreled" and "testing") and became a symbol of the people's hard hearts. Psalm 95 refers back to this grumbling and complaining against God as the essence of a rebellious, hard heart and the reason why the people did not enter the promised land:

> Today, if you hear his voice,
>> do not harden your hearts, as at Meribah,
>> as on the day at Massah in the wilderness,
> when your fathers put me to the test
>> and put me to the proof, though they had seen my
>> work.
> For forty years I loathed that generation
>> and said, "They are a people who go astray in
>> their heart,
>> and they have not known my ways."
> Therefore I swore in my wrath,
>> "They shall not enter my rest." (vv. 7–11)

The author of Hebrews extensively meditates on this very passage as the basis of his exhortation to follow Christ by faith all the way to heaven (Heb. 3–4). To "harden your heart" through the unbelief of grumbling and complaining against him is rebellion.

Complaining Is Opposed to the Entire Work of Conversion

Burroughs is especially powerful here. He leads his readers through a step-by-step analysis of the heart work the Holy Spirit does in us, resulting in our conversion to Christ, and goes on to show how discontentment and complaining (which he calls "murmuring") are opposed to each step. The six steps Burroughs describes are (1) seeing the greatness of your sin, (2) seeing the greatness of Christ, (3) turning away from this world's pleasures and toward Christ, (4) casting yourself fully on Christ, (5) submitting yourself to Christ's kingly reign, and (6) making a lasting covenant with God that you are his possession.

Let's look at each of these points and how they are affected by our murmuring and complaining as we either forget about our discontentment and allow it to stay or willfully turn away from contentment.

1. Murmuring forgets how deeply sinful we were apart from Christ, how we owed ten thousand talents (Matt. 18:24). Any one of those sins unatoned for was worthy of sinking us eternally in hell. Christ covered all that sin by his blood shed on the cross. Now, because of some minor afflictions, we who are still walking the earth and not condemned to hell are complaining against God.

2. Complaining forgets how stunningly majestic and glorious a savior Christ is, how he is our treasure and our portion. In our murmuring we are effectively saying to Christ that his death on the cross and his resurrection for us are insufficient; we must have a little more, or we cannot be happy.

   Imagine taking one of your kids to the Grand Canyon. As you approach the breathtaking rim and see all the colors and the awesome display of immensity, the child is angry and frustrated at the fact that their handheld computer game has run out of battery power. Given the expense of paying for the plane flight and all the joy you have in revealing this stunning beauty, for them to be angry about something so petty is incredibly irksome. You might have the strong urge to grab the game and hurl it as far as possible into the canyon! But you don't want to pollute the place, so you confiscate the device for the rest of the trip. That is how our short-sighted, pathetic complaints look to our God, who has spread out before us a spiritual vista of infinite worth in Christ, who is "the radiance of the glory of God and the exact imprint of his nature" (Heb. 1:3). Why isn't his glory enough for us?

3. Complaining forgets the fact that, at conversion, we turned away from the world and all its creature comforts, allurements, pleasures, and empty promises and chose instead the kingdom of God. We were taught that to save our life in this world is to lose it, but to lose our life for Christ is to find it (Luke 17:33). In the verse just prior to this, Jesus warns us, "Remember Lot's wife" (v. 32). She looked back longingly at her former life in Sodom and was turned into a pillar of salt. When we grumble and complain about some earthly situation, we have forgotten that, by the cross of Christ, the world should be crucified to us, as we are to the world (Gal. 6:14).

4. Complaining forgets that we have cast ourselves fully on Christ as our eternal source of joy. He has become for us a fountain of living water springing up to eternal life (John 4:14). Having come to him, we should never thirst again. But here we are, thirsting after something that God is not choosing to give us, effectively saying that Christ is no longer satisfying to us.

5. In conversion, we are submitting fully to Christ as our King. As we've seen, this is precisely what Christ commands by these words: "Take my yoke upon you, and learn from me. . . . For my yoke is easy, and my burden is light" (Matt. 11:29–30). When we complain, we have reversed course and are throwing off his kingly yoke by openly questioning his wise rulership of our lives.

6. In conversion we have made an eternal covenant with God, saying, "I am yours and you are mine." This was always God's central desire in our salvation: that he would be God to us and that we would be his covenant people, his treasured possession. Complaining attacks that covenant with bitter acid, as though we regret ever having made it to begin with. It's like we no longer wish to be married to our heavenly Spouse.

Complaining Is Unworthy of a Child of the King

When King David's wicked son, Amnon, lay on his bed moaning and sullen because he could not sleep with his half sister Tamar, his shrewd friend Jonadab said, "Why are you, the king's son, so miserable every morning?" (2 Sam. 13:4 CSB). The basic assumption is that such obvious misery is utterly incongruous with being the king's son. Princes are lavishly cared for! So how is it even possible that the king's son should be so unhappy?

Now Prince Amnon's desire was utterly corrupt, as are many of the desires that afflict our souls. And even if the desires are not in any way corrupt—the desire for the healing of a loved one, for example, or the desire for a Christian spouse—it is every bit as wrong for those who are heirs of the King of the Universe to be miserable day after day over any earthly issue. To complain is to forget how rich you are as an heir of the King.

Complaining Forgets the Many Blessings You Have Already Received

It is true that the best blessings we get in the gospel are spiritual, as we just noted. But complaining forgets how many blessings God has already lavished on us for years on earth and how many he pours out on us in the midst of our afflictions.

A number of years ago on Thanksgiving Day I sat on a porch with my son, Calvin, and challenged us both to come up with one hundred things to thank God for. We would alternate, so each of us was responsible for fifty. Anything was fair game, from lofty spiritual blessings to small earthly blessings like Calvin's football card collection.

I will never forget how sweet that time was. It was rainy, and we thanked God for the rain, the very thing unbelievers never thank him for (Matt. 5:45). The lavish feast we were about to eat gave us lots of details to thank God for: turkey, mashed potatoes, gravy, sweet potato casserole, green beans, three different pies, a hard-working mom who was laboring to cook it all for us. When we whine and complain about something we are missing, we are forgetting all of God's benefits. And that is a grave dishonor to him.

Complaining Sets a Bad Example

We were meant to be a light shining in a dark place as we hold forth the word of life to others. But Paul says we must do everything without grumbling or arguing in order that we may shine that light (Phil. 2:14–16).

Someone is always watching. And when we murmur against God, we are dragging people down. It might be a wife or husband who has to put up with years of a spouse's caustic attitude toward life. Remember that Christian contentment is a "sweet" frame of spirit, as opposed to bitter or sour. A discontent person is wretched to be around. However funny it is to read Eeyore's lines in *Winnie the Pooh*, inwardly we're groaning with memories of people "just like that." What should make us wince is to realize that we ourselves are people "just like that."

God has put us on display in front of everyone we know, but especially our spouse and our children. We can make life bitter for the person we embraced on our wedding day and strongly tempt that loving soul to discontentment as well. Not only that, but if you have children, think of them. They have been watching your example for years, quietly drinking in how to react to "any and every circumstance." When you complain, you are training them to follow your bad example.

Beyond this is the role we have in the lives of watching Christian brothers and sisters. God has ordained the church to be a disciple-making organism. There are two patterns of discipleship by which we are being conformed to Christ: the pattern of sound doctrine (2 Tim. 1:13) and the pattern of godly example (Phil. 3:17). Paul says boldly, "What you have learned and received and heard and seen in me—practice these things, and the God of peace will be with you" (Phil. 4:9). Role modeling in the Christian church is essential to God's plan of discipleship. But when we murmur, complain, and whine, we are polluting those watching us. We are undoing any good that the Lord would have us do.

Complaining Makes No Unbeliever Want to Be Like You

By far the most significant audience, however, is unbelievers. As we noted in the last chapter, Christ has ordained that we are "the light of the world," "a city set on a hill," and has said that he puts that light "on a stand, and it gives light to all in the house" (Matt. 5:14–15). This world of ours is swimming in a sea of misery, disease, tragedy, pain, disappointment, suffering, and death. The unbelievers are "without hope and without God in the world" (Eph. 2:12 CSB).

God may well have orchestrated our affliction, suffering, chronic illness, natural disaster, or whatever to give us the right to speak from a platform of hope to lost people suffering the exact same miseries. But if we are bitterly complaining, why would they ask us to give a reason for the hope that's inside us (1 Pet. 3:15)? We don't seem to have any! They don't need lessons on complaining. God has orchestrated a costly platform from which we can witness, through our suffering, and in our complaining we are missing that golden opportunity. The best thing we can do is learn the lessons from the past and resolve that if God should ever put us in such an arena of pain, we will glorify God and point lost people to the light of hope.

The Excuses of a Complaining Heart

One of the geniuses of Puritan preaching and writing was how thoroughly they probed the inner workings of the human heart. Burroughs worked carefully through a list of excuses that sinners will make to escape the conviction they are feeling for complaining against God.[4] I borrowed some of his while adding a few of my own.

"I'm Not Complaining; I'm Just Venting"

In the "therapeutic" excuse for complaining, the person claims the need to blow off steam, get it off their chest so they don't blow up later. This is a transparent ruse of the sinful nature. When we speak negative words to another person, we're merely showing distress and dislike for what is going on around us. But Scripture demonstrates a godly pattern of respectfully pouring out our heart to the Lord, casting our burden on him because he cares for us (1 Pet. 5:7). And that's our therapy.

Another therapy is the godly meditations that I have already recommended. The Lord Jesus Christ is the Great Physician, and he can cure us. There isn't anything wrong with telling the facts of our affliction to brothers and sisters in Christ so they can pray for us or meet our need. Yet when we complain, we marinate in the details of the affliction right in the presence of another. This lie of the heart can be healed with truth. As we are speaking, are we displaying a sweet, inward, quiet, gracious frame of spirit that is freely submitting to and delighting in God's wise and fatherly disposal in this specific condition? Or are we just complaining?

"God Has Abandoned Me"

Sometimes people who are complaining are saying that God has abandoned them, that God is quiet, or that God doesn't give them any inner peace or answer any of their prayers. Do we not see what an evil thing it is to say that, because of our affliction, God has broken his promise, "I will never leave you nor forsake you" (Heb. 13:5)?

God told us what to do when we are facing trials of various kinds: "Count it all joy," knowing that God is working in our soul to make us "perfect and complete, lacking in nothing" (James 1:2, 4). Christ has already promised us, "In this world you will have trouble." But he also said in that same verse, "In me you may have peace," and "Take heart! I have overcome the world" (John 16:33). How is it, then, that Satan has deceived us into believing, when trouble comes, that God has abandoned us?

Press through the dimness of your soul in prayer. Fight for joy! Claim the promises! In this way, God means to strengthen your faith as never before. Many godly servants of Christ have faced extreme temptations toward spiritual depression. Adoniram Judson dug his own grave and sat by it for a while after the death of his wife and daughter.[5] But even these extreme times of depression can be overcome by an appeal to the promises and presence of Christ.

"You Don't Know . . ."

People can try our souls, no doubt. People can often be the instrument of the devil (2 Tim. 2:26), tempting us away from contentment. We might even feel justified in responding to someone who urges us to trust God and stop complaining by saying, "You don't know how annoying and distressing that person is. If you had a wife (or a husband, boss, neighbor, teenager, etc.) like I have, you would be exasperated too!"

But the essence of Christian contentment is that it is totally independent of any created thing. Remember, the word is "self-sufficiency," which we know means "God-sufficiency."

Having God, we don't need our spouse or boss or neighbor or teenager to be any certain way. If your spouse is miserable and nagging you constantly, that is no excuse for ceasing to walk in the Spirit yourself. If your boss only criticizes your performance and never sees the extra time you put into that project or the nights you worked at home to finish it, that is no excuse for becoming bitter and failing to praise God. If your neighbor continues to have loud parties till late at night, even though you have asked nicely and repeatedly for him to change, you do not have any right to stop peacefully trusting in God's providence. And if your teenager is struggling with life and is immaturely rebelling against almost all of your directions, you are not thereby given permission by the Holy Spirit to let go of sweet contentment. As a matter of fact, it is precisely by being strong in contentment in just such times as those that you will most likely effect a positive outcome.

Fundamental to making daily progress toward Christlikeness is taking responsibility for your own sin. You have been set free from sin by Christ (Rom. 6:18). This means you never need to sin again! It also means no other being—no demon, no human—can ever compel us to sin. Ever. Therefore, whenever we do sin, it's our fault. We must take responsibility for our contentment in the power of the Spirit.

"I Never Expected This"

Some people make excuses for their complaining by saying the affliction was far different than they ever thought would come upon them. It has come at them from a different angle and has laid them low. They didn't see it coming. But by saying this, they are just admitting that they were ill prepared and that they thought some aspect of their life was exempt from anything negative happening. Like new homeowners who are so delighted with their new home that they see no need at all for fire insurance.

Nothing earthly is secure. All things that we see with our eyes are temporary. Be ready for anything to be taken from you, and resolve that you will praise the Lord no matter what happens. Everything we have is really his, and we have it on loan with an expectation of return on his investment. He can take it back any time without being guilty of injustice. We should do a spiritual inventory ahead of time and give it all up to God in prayer.

"You've Never Experienced Anything Like What I'm Going Through"

This is a particularly harsh excuse for complaining. It is often said by a grieving person to someone who is trying to help, perhaps someone who said something like, "I know how you feel." Admittedly, this is not the best thing to say to a grieving person. But when that person responds so bitterly—"You have no idea how I feel! You've never been through anything like this!"—it can end up silencing a caring friend who would like to offer comfort. More famously, one could say, "Nobody knows the trouble I've seen." But such an assertion sounds a little arrogant if considered plainly on the printed page, apart from a genuine circumstance.

First of all, every circumstance of suffering is in one sense unique, since it involves specific personalities and details that can never be perfectly repeated. So by that logic, no one can ever show compassion to any other person. Not even a parent whose child died of the same disease that took the life of someone else's child knows *exactly* what the other family is going through. On the other hand, "No temptation has overtaken you that is not *common to man.* God is faithful, and he will not let you be tempted beyond your ability" (1 Cor. 10:13). Our brothers and sisters all over the world are going through the same sufferings (1 Pet. 5:9). And there are some in the world who have suffered far more than any of us ever have. It is better to keep our afflictions in eternal perspective, as Paul said: "For this light momentary affliction is preparing for us an eternal weight of glory beyond all comparison" (2 Cor. 4:17). And Paul's credentials of suffering are among the greatest in the history of the church.

"I Don't Deserve This"

Sometimes people complain that their sufferings are unjust. This was Job's complaint (Job 27:2), as we've noted. But God later rebuked Job for trying to justify himself by questioning God's justice (40:8). Job repented in sackcloth and ashes. There's only one truly just circumstance for us sinners, and that is eternal death in hell. Anything we get on earth is infinitely better than we deserve. It is our pride that makes us forget that. Instead of complaining, we ought to thank God for the marvelous grace he is showing us in Christ to make our sufferings prepare us for eternal glory far weightier than anything we've experienced on earth (Rom. 8:18). And none of us deserves that!

"Yes, I Admit I'm Complaining . . . but I Can't Help Myself"

This is perhaps the most honest of all the complaints. But it shows a fundamental denial of the very fact I just cited a moment ago: Christ, by his death and his resurrection, has set us free forever from all sin, if we are Christians (Rom. 6:1–4, 18). Satan can never force us to sin again, ever.

No single temptation will ever come against us throughout the rest of our lives that we must obey. We can kill all temptations by the power of the Spirit. Though we will never be fully and finally free of any sin pattern in this world, yet little by little we can make sin habits gradually weaker by starving them to death. That's what Romans 6 teaches so powerfully: "We know that our old self was crucified with him in order that the body of sin might be brought to nothing [*katargēthē*], so that we would no longer be enslaved to sin" (v. 6). The person we were positionally in Adam died in Christ the moment we were converted. As a result, the "body of sin"—our sin habits as wired in our body and our brain—can little by little be rendered powerless. The Greek word *katargeō*, which I just translated as "brought to nothing," could also mean "nullified," "rendered powerless," or "starved to death" by long-standing denial of that sin. Just as we learned the old habit of systematic complaining, now we can learn new habits of consistent contentment by the power of the Spirit.

Old wicked habits die through starvation, and new godly habits grow through obedience: "Just as you once presented your members as slaves to impurity and to lawlessness leading to more lawlessness, so now present your members as slaves to righteousness leading to sanctification" (Rom. 6:19).

In Christ and by the Spirit, put complaining to death and learn more and more the habits of contentment.

In this chapter, I have desired to stimulate us to see how repulsive our complaining can be, so that we will be moved to delight more and more in God's wise plan, and to humbly submit ourselves to it day by day.

nine

CONTENTMENT
IN SUFFERING

On Sunday, January 25, 1736, John Wesley sailed in a wooden vessel into a hurricane in the middle of the Atlantic Ocean. The small ship rose "to the heavens above" and fell "to hell beneath" on the heaving waves.[1] The winds ripped at the sails with howling shrieks, and every ten minutes a shock would hit the stern or sides so powerfully that it seemed the ship was about to be broken in pieces. At that point in his life, Wesley did not yet know salvation by grace through faith in Christ alone, and he was terrified of death. But on board that ship were a group of Moravian Christians, and their supernatural calm in the midst of that storm displayed a spiritual stability in salvation that he did not yet possess. They were singing praises to God in a Sunday service:

In the midst of the psalm wherewith their service began, the sea broke over, split the main-sail in pieces, covered the ship, and poured in between the decks, as if the great deep had already swallowed us up. A terrible screaming began among the [sailors]. The Germans calmly sung on. I asked one of them afterwards, "Were you not afraid?" He answered, "I thank God, no." I asked, "But were not your women and children afraid?" He replied, mildly, "No; our women and children are not afraid to die." From them I went to the crying, trembling [sailors], and pointed out to them the difference in the hour of trial, between him that feareth God, and him that feareth him not.[2]

The supernatural contentment these Moravian Christians displayed, not just in the storm but at all times, had a powerful effect on Wesley and eventually led him to find true salvation in Christ. Their behavior in the storm was no aberration; it was the way they lived every day of their lives. Wesley saw that they regularly accepted menial and disgusting tasks that no one else would do, saying that "it was good for their proud hearts" and that "their loving Savior" had done more for them.[3] If they were attacked or thrown to the ground, they would walk away with no show of anger or revenge. And when the terrifying storm came, they simply continued to act in that circumstance as they did in every circumstance. In the end, their supernatural contentment revealed to him his own spiritual poverty and was instrumental in his later conversion.[4]

There is no time in a Christian's weary and painful pilgrimage to heaven when contentment is so precious and yet so hard to come by as during times of suffering. And the greater the suffering, the more this divine and supernatural contentment will be vital to our souls, glorifying to God, and fruitful in eternity. As we saw at the beginning of this book, it is in the depths of the earth, in the unspeakable heat and pressures of tectonic activity, that the rare jewels we treasure are formed. It is there, hidden from human view, that common carbon turns into fiery diamond. So it is also with radiant Christian maturity.

God wills to have it so. And we know it too. The longer we live, the more this world seems an alien and hostile place, filled with dangers to our souls. The older we get, the more we see our indwelling sins and the pain they cause God and others. The more hospital beds and funeral parlors we visit, the more starkly do we become aware that no one makes it through this valley of the shadow of death unscathed. Our time is coming, if it hasn't already begun.

Perhaps you are reading this chapter right now with intense interest because God has struck your world with a sharp and painful blow. You are still reeling and asking questions from the depths of your being. You yearn for a little help, a lifeline to keep you from sinking into despair. Or perhaps you are just reading the next chapter in this book; you are young, healthy, good-looking, successful, optimistic, and looking forward to a prosperous Christian life with abundant rewards. You are aware that there is much suffering in the world, but it hasn't hit you yet. May the meditations of this chapter prepare you for the hammer and chisel that the Master Sculptor must bring upon your soul to shape you for eternal glory. The chiseling will be deeply painful. O that you may not charge God with any wrongdoing as he works!

Answering the Charges of an Angry World

The world of unbelievers does not know this kind of supernatural hope and joy during suffering. If anything, the fact that there is such overwhelming human agony and death is powerful evidence to them that a good, all-powerful, loving God cannot possibly exist. As Tim Keller discusses in *The Reason for God*, Christians making a defense for their faith inevitably have to answer this charge on behalf of God: "If a good and powerful God exists, he would not allow pointless evil, but because there is so much unjustifiable pointless evil in the world, the traditional good and powerful God could not exist." Keller points out that the flaw in that thinking is the arrogance in humans being so confident in their judgments, as if it's valid to say, "If our minds can't plumb the depths of the universe for good answers to suffering, well, then, there can't be any!"[5]

Yet these are the kinds of charges unbelievers seem to make after every major natural disaster or private tragedy. David Bentley Hart wrote these powerfully angry words in the *Wall Street Journal* after a devastating tsunami in the Indian Ocean in December of 2004: "When confronted by the sheer savage immensity of worldly suffering—when we see the entire littoral rim of the Indian Ocean strewn with tens of thousands of corpses, a third of them children's—no Christian is licensed to utter odious banalities about God's inscrutable counsels or blasphemous suggestions that all this mysteriously serves God's ends."[6]

No Christian apologist wrestled so intelligently and personally with the problem of suffering as did C. S. Lewis. He made it plain in his classic *Mere Christianity* that the very questions being asked about justice, evil, and suffering tend to be arguments *for* the existence of God: "My argument against God was that the universe seemed cruel and unjust. But how had I gotten the idea of 'just' and 'unjust'? . . . What was I comparing this universe with when I called it unjust? . . . Consequently atheism turns out to be too simple."[7]

In 1940, Lewis also wrote a powerful book, *The Problem of Pain*, to dig deeper into this perplexing issue. The basic problem his book sought to answer was, "If God were good, he would make his creatures perfectly happy; and if he were almighty, he would be able to do as he wished. But his creatures are not perfectly happy. Therefore God lacks either goodness, or power, or both."[8] Lewis's answer is that God uses pain as his most powerful tool to wean sinners from the woefully inadequate views of happiness that our flesh pursues: "We can ignore even pleasure. But pain insists upon being attended to. God whispers to us in our pleasures, speaks in our conscience, but shouts in our pains: it is his megaphone to rouse a deaf world."[9]

I want to be so bold as to expand on Lewis here for a moment. This megaphone of pain cannot be heard by a truly deaf person; neither can it be heard by a truly dead person. The unbelieving world is "dead in [its] trespasses and sins" (Eph. 2:1). Spiritually dead people will not hear God's whispers in pleasure, his speaking in conscience, or even his shouting through a megaphone in pain.

We Christians are alive, not dead, and we are not entirely deaf. But like the man who saw "people . . . like trees walking" (Mark 8:24 CSB) and was (initially) partially healed from blindness by Jesus, we are partially healed from deafness—we can hear somewhat dimly and fuzzily in pleasures and conscience. The megaphone of pain is intended for Christians, and it is only effective for them. That's where Christian contentment comes in. We must put Christian contentment on display before this angry, indignant, suffering world to show that the true answer is Christ.

"Why, O Lord?": Seven Insights from Scripture

When we are going through intense suffering, the most natural question to ask is, "Why, O Lord? Why did you do this?" Why did you take my little boy? Why didn't you heal my wife? Why didn't you protect our home from the hurricane? Why did my daughter die in the car crash, and the drunk driver walk away without a scratch?

I well remember the night my wife, Christi, came home from the hospital after major neck fusion surgery. She had been a remarkable soldier through some of the worst pain of her life, but now it was two or three in the morning and her shoulder muscles were having aggressive spasms on both sides of her healing incision. I was holding her from behind, trying to get her shoulders in a less painful position. With tears streaming down her face, she begged me, "Make it stop!" I said to her, "I can't. And the One who can is choosing not to." God could have moved his little finger and made the muscle spasms stop immediately. And eventually they did stop, by the mercy of God. But he willed her to undergo that pain for an hour or more. Other people endure life-altering trauma to their bodies, like Joni Eareckson Tada, who, at age seventeen, dove off a bridge into shallow water in the Chesapeake Bay, broke her neck, and was paralyzed. For the rest of her life.

In both cases, some could say these sufferings happened "seemingly for no reason at all." But God always has a reason for what he does and for what he does not do. And it is biblically acceptable for us to ask him, "Why, O Lord?!"

What follows is a series of helpful practical steps that Scripture commends to us to enable us to be content in times of affliction and earthly sorrow.

Ask for Wisdom

As we saw in chapter 3, there are many anguished prayers to God in Scripture, all of them inspired by the Holy Spirit and recorded for our instruction. God wants us to pour out our hearts to him in respectful, faith-filled, and passionate words. So when the trial starts and your heart is being assaulted by doubts and fears, that is the time to come to God and ask for wisdom. It is very significant that, after telling us to "count it all joy" (James 1:2) whenever we go through trials of any magnitude, James urges us to ask God for wisdom: "If any of you lacks wisdom, let him ask God, who gives generously to all without reproach, and it will be given him" (v. 5). It is reasonable in context to see a strong link between the two topics: first, the benefits of experiencing trials, and second, how this specific trial fits into God's overall plan and his plan for your life. Knowing that the suffering is not random but has a specific place in God's intricate providence is immensely comforting.

Rest in God's Goodness

Few stories in the Bible are as powerfully moving as the account of Joseph and his many sufferings. Joseph was sold into slavery by his jealous brothers (Gen. 37:27) and then was wrongly accused of sexual assault by Potiphar's wife, resulting in his unjust imprisonment (39:7–20). While Joseph was in prison, he successfully interpreted the dreams of two high-ranking officials in Pharaoh's court. But the official who should have put in a word for him with Pharaoh forgot, and Joseph stayed in prison two more years. Two whole years of his life . . . waiting for the plan of God to unfold! But at just the right time, Pharaoh had two mysterious dreams, and the forgetful official finally remembered Joseph and recommended him to Pharaoh. Joseph accurately interpreted the dreams, predicting that seven years of plenty would be followed by seven years of famine.

Pharaoh saw Joseph's astonishing qualities and put him in charge of all of Egypt. In the course of time, Joseph's brothers came to Egypt to buy food because of the famine, and God used Joseph's wisdom and power to save his family from starvation. After the death of their father, Jacob, Joseph's brothers were afraid that he would now move to exact his vengeance on them. But Joseph spoke some of the most profound words in the Bible on the providence of God: "'As for you, you meant evil against me, but God meant it for good, to bring it about that many people should be kept alive, as they are today. So do not fear; I will provide for you and your little ones.' Thus he comforted them and spoke kindly to them" (Gen. 50:20–21).

Notice that Joseph acknowledges their evil intent and doesn't excuse it. But he sees God's higher purpose and bows humbly and in awe before it. God "meant it" for good. It was not an accident, nor merely an act of random evil. Notice also that his theology of God's sovereign decree frees him from all bitterness; he spoke kindly to them and sweetly met their needs. What a display of supernatural contentment!

This is a powerful example for all of us in times of suffering. God's wise plan was unfolding, including the saving of Jacob and the patriarchs of the twelve tribes of Israel from starvation. And his plan would extend far beyond this, including the amazing exodus from slavery in Egypt under Moses, all of it predicted to Abram in Genesis 15:13–15. Joseph trusted in God enough to see his goodness in these apparently evil events. The human side was evil, but because God is good, only good can come from him.

When we are going through immense suffering, we can rest in God's goodness as he unfolds his inscrutable plans. Jacob blessed Joseph with these words: "The archers bitterly attacked him, shot at him, and harassed him severely, yet his bow remained unmoved; his arms were made agile by the hands of the Mighty One of Jacob" (Gen. 49:23–24). Joseph was *strong* in the Lord, and his arms remained "agile" or "supple," not stiff or hard. This is a poetical description of contentment. If his long and unjust sufferings had made him bitter, he would not have been able to do what God wanted him to do in Pharaoh's court. If he had come out of prison complaining about his brothers or Potiphar, he might even have been returned to prison. But his sweet spirit enabled him to save Egypt, as well as his family, and kept him from bitterness toward his brothers. His sense of the providence of God was essential to all of this.

Expect Suffering

One of the sweetest verses in the Bible tells us what to expect in the new heaven and new earth: "He will wipe away every tear from their eyes, and death shall be no more, neither shall there be mourning, nor crying, nor pain anymore, for the former things have passed away" (Rev. 21:4). But we're not there yet. Jesus warned us, "You will have suffering in this world" (John 16:33 CSB). In this present age, there is a flood of tears, mourning, crying, pain . . . and death. In the next world, there will be none of those things. Death is "the last enemy" (1 Cor. 15:26), and Jesus will most certainly destroy it. But not yet.

Therefore, in this world we must expect suffering, sickness, pain, and death. We should not be surprised when they come, for this is the very thing God warned Adam would happen if he ate from the tree (Gen. 2:17). So when we cry out to God, "Why, O Lord?!" we must realize that part of the answer is that, because of Adam's sin, this is the very nature of this present age. God will occasionally protect us from pain and suffering, but it is appointed to each one of us to die once (Heb. 9:27). Yet we suffer in hope, because another world is coming in which all this grief will come to an eternal end.

Acknowledge Our Limited Perspective

The unfolding story of redemptive history may be likened to a magnificent tapestry, woven skillfully with many colored threads to produce a final product that will take our breath away when we see it in all its heavenly glory. Our times of suffering are like many dark-colored threads that are essential to the design.

In 1987, I went on a mission trip to Pakistan to minister to Afghan refugees who had fled from the Russian invasion. These people were destitute and desperately in need of a better economic future. We were involved in setting up job training for many of them in the manufacture of Persian rugs, a lucrative trade that could meet their needs very well. In the process of connecting them with craftsmen who could train them, we found ourselves in a high-end shop in Islamabad with extremely expensive antique Persian rugs. One in particular was from the 1920s, made of silk. The merchant taught us what characterized a rug of the highest quality. He showed us especially the back of the rug, and displayed the overwhelmingly dense number of tiny knots of silk thread that the craftsman had tied one at a time over six decades earlier. It was impressive, but the design on the back was incomprehensible. It was not until he turned it over and put it on a display rack in the sunlight that the breathtaking scene on the carpet came to life: a Persian prince riding through a mountain pass on a white horse with a long plume coming from his hat.

Our lives are like that Persian rug—skillfully woven in an incomprehensible pattern of pain and pleasure, days of darkness and days of bright sunshine. The Craftsman is God, and he alone has the final picture in his mind. We will see it in heaven, but now it sometimes seems to make no sense at all.

Accept That Suffering Can Sanctify

Scripture makes it plain that our own suffering is essential to our final salvation from sin. Now we must be clear: we are not justified by our suffering, as some medieval monks believed when they whipped themselves until their backs bled and thought that by this act of suffering they could escape eternal torment. We are justified by faith in Christ's suffering

138

on the cross (Rom. 3:24–25). However, our own suffering is essential to our sanctification, especially in weaning us from earthly idols. As C. S. Lewis wrote, pain is God's megaphone to wean us from the earth. Before we go through pain and suffering, we are often so entranced by the world that we can barely hear his still, small voice. We treasure the things of the world far too much. We define our blessedness in the meager terms of prosperity, physical health, success, family, friends, and the like. God often scarcely makes the radar screen. God needs to wean us from earthly idols to cause us to focus entirely on him. And pain is often a powerfully effective tool in killing our idols.

Anticipate Our Eternal Glory

Paul says that "this light momentary affliction is preparing for us an eternal weight of glory beyond all comparison" (2 Cor. 4:17). The word "preparing" could also be translated "achieving," "working," or "producing." Not only are the afflictions light and momentary compared with eternal glory, they are *essential* in preparing us for that glory. By our earthly sufferings, we are being conformed more and more to Christ, as we just noted a moment ago, but we are also enabled to do mighty works of sacrificial love for Christ that he will reward with crowns of glory that we will wear forever (1 Thess. 2:19; 1 Pet. 5:4). Jesus said that if we are persecuted for Christ, we should rejoice and be glad because we will receive a great reward in heaven. So also any loving sacrificial service in daily life will enhance our heavenly glory. Cheerful, faith-filled suffering in this life is eternally rewarded in the next.

Share Hope

As I have said earlier, God may well orchestrate immense suffering in our lives to put our faith on display. Christ calls us "the light of the world" and says he will put us on a stand to give light to everyone in the house (Matt. 5:14–16). This world is dark with misery and suffering, and only the light of the gospel can push back the darkness. Our hope-filled suffering in the ICU or the funeral parlor can shine to lost people who are watching us closely. In more extreme settings, God has chosen to use the supernatural courage of martyrs to spread the gospel of Christ. Tertullian said famously, "The blood of martyrs is seed" (that is, for the church).[10] Paul says that we are considered "sheep for the slaughter" (Rom. 8:36 KJV). Our commitment to spread the gospel among unsaved coworkers or lost Muslims in the Middle East will be costly, but glorious.

Imitating the Faith of Heroes

God has sprinkled godly examples of supernatural contentment in suffering like so many diamonds in the records of history. Hebrews 11 gives us a Hall of Faith and urges us to walk reverently through that corridor of time, to pause and study the examples of faith-filled heroes who lived before us. The next chapters go on to recommend our imitation of these faithful ones: "Therefore, since we are surrounded by so great a cloud of witnesses, let us also lay aside every weight, and sin which clings so closely, and let us run with endurance the race that is set before us" (12:1). "Remember your leaders, those who spoke to you the word of God.

Consider the outcome of their way of life, and *imitate their faith*" (13:7). Hebrews 11 is filled with the courageous and otherworldly perspective of these heroes, men and women who suffered and died without receiving the promises, but only seeing them from a distance, and who "acknowledged that they were strangers and exiles on the earth" (11:13). God has prepared a city and a country for such people where they will dwell forever (11:13–16).

Church history has continued since those days, and the Hall of Faith has had many radiant men and women added to it. The "great cloud of witnesses" that surrounds us is far greater and more glorious than it was two thousand years ago. I could mention the history of missions in which amazingly bold servants of Christ, both men and women, laid down their lives to bring the gospel to the sugar plantations of the West Indies, to the lion-infested plains of Africa, to the steamy jungles of head-hunting tribes in the Amazon and Irian Jaya, to the teeming cities of the Far East, or to the terrifying prisons in Communist and Muslim lands. That history is unspeakably glorious, and well worth recounting, because none of those advances could have been made without loving, cheerful sacrifice. Those courageous brothers and sisters paid a cost far higher than most of us will ever know.

These accounts of extreme suffering for the spread of the gospel rightly should take first place in this chapter. Yet because most of us aren't called to martyrdom in our country or even to board planes to serve as career missionaries, most of our times of extreme suffering will come in the normal course of painful diseases or shocking accidents. That is why I want to call to the witness stand Jonathan and Sarah

Edwards, Tim and Madge Pyrant, and Larry and Alana Parrish, all of whom faced this bitter providence of suffering with heroic faith, with admirable displays of Christian contentment. May we sit at their feet and drink in their wisdom.

Jonathan and Sarah Edwards

Jonathan Edwards (1703–58) was arguably the greatest American theologian of all time. His wife, Sarah (1710–58), was an amazingly patient, wise, and godly woman who was every bit his equal in Christian maturity. God chose by a bitter providence to put her character on display for all time. While Jonathan was away from her, preparing to become president of the College of New Jersey (later called Princeton), he received a smallpox inoculation, as many did in those days. But it went horribly wrong. His throat swelled up with the disease, his fever raged, and he soon died (March 22, 1758). Sarah received news of his death and wrote this timeless letter to their daughter, Esther. Even now, after having read it countless times, I cannot read it again without tears in my eyes.

> What shall I say: A holy and good God has covered us with a dark cloud. O that we may kiss the rod, and lay our hands on our mouths! The Lord has done it. He has made me adore his goodness that we had him so long. But my God lives; and he has my heart. O what a legacy my husband, and your father, has left to us! We are all given to God: and there I am and love to be. Your ever affectionate mother, Sarah Edwards.[11]

What a hero she was! Has there ever been a clearer statement of Christian contentment? Here is a godly woman who deeply loved her husband and has now learned that she would never see him again in this world. This was her reaction. She is well aware of her sorrow; she feels deeply the pain, for she speaks of a dark cloud. She embraces the doctrine of God's sovereign disposal, for it is God who has chosen to cover her with the dark cloud. She says clearly, "The Lord has done it." But she does not charge him with wrongdoing. Instead, she calls him "holy and good." Furthermore, she is clinging to him as her living treasure, for she says, "My God lives; and he has my heart." Her true delight is God, not Jonathan. "We are all given to God: and there I am and love to be." She is well aware that she is on display, even while she writes to her daughter. She wants Esther to know that "we are all given to God." She is deeply thankful for the past goodness of God in having such an incredibly godly and fruitful husband as she did. She is mindful of the legacy Jonathan has left to future generations of Christians. Yet it was very personal to her and to Esther, for she calls him "my husband" and "your father."

But for me, by far the most amazing thing she writes are these words: "O that we may kiss the rod, and lay our hands on our mouths!" What incredible maturity this reveals! The rod is the chastening rod of reproof by a loving heavenly Father. No matter how godly she is, she is well aware that there is still the deep-seated corruption of indwelling sin and that God uses these bitter moments to drive the sin out of our souls. But that only happens if we "kiss the rod," if we willingly accept and submit to what God wills. We must see such painful providences as part of God's wise and fatherly plan to sanctify us through and through and thereby fit us for heaven. But she knows her own weakness and, like Job, says, "I lay my hand on my mouth" (Job 40:4). The tongue is a "restless evil, full of deadly poison" (James 3:8). It will speak the hidden corruptions of our hearts in bitter accusations against God if we do not "set a guard . . . over the door of [our] lips" (Ps. 141:3).

This timeless letter is truly one of the greatest moments of Christian contentment in church history. Amazingly, Esther never read the letter, for she died of a fever before it could reach her. And Sarah herself would join her beloved husband in glory that same year. But her letter is a legacy every bit as rich as the works her husband authored.

I want also to add the amazing testimony concerning Jonathan himself. Dr. Shippen, his attending physician, wrote this account to Sarah of how her husband died:

> And never did any mortal man more fully and clearly evidence the sincerity of all his professions, by one continued, universal, calm, cheerful resignation, and patient submission to the divine will, through every stage of his disease, than he; not so much as one discontented expression, nor the least appearance of murmuring through the whole. And never did any person expire with more perfect freedom from pain;— not so much as one distorted hair—but in the most proper sense of the words, he really fell asleep. Death had certainly lost its sting, as to him.[12]

O that we would study these testimonies and prepare to face death—either our own or that of a loved one—with the same display of faith-filled Christian contentment! O that we would die well!

Tim and Madge Pyrant

It is likely that you have heard of Jonathan and Sarah Edwards. But Tim and Madge Pyrant are heroes of the faith you probably have not yet heard of. Tim was a member of our church, First Baptist Church of Durham. On June 6, 2015, I had the privilege of performing his funeral. He had fought valiantly for two years against a brain tumor, a glioblastoma, which is a type of tumor that is almost always fatal. Tim's faith-filled manner of living, fighting, and dying will stay with me the rest of my life.

Soon after he was diagnosed, Tim began keeping a journal. John Piper wrote a booklet called *Don't Waste Your Cancer*, urging people to maximize God's glory in the process of living in pain and possibly dying.[13] Tim Pyrant took that to heart and certainly didn't waste his cancer. He was a bright, shining light in the cancer ward at Duke University Hospital, where he was treated. He was consistently joyful and trusting, openly speaking of Christ every chance he got. But the words of his journal, which his loving wife, Madge, allowed me to read at the funeral, shine the brightest. Look what he wrote when he first heard the diagnosis:

> 9/26/13 Trying to understand why I have cancer. I am very remiss not to concentrate on why God has blessed me with cancer! Like a beautiful diamond cut by the master jeweler himself, I see many facets (reasons) God has done this marvelous thing!
>
> Facet #1: To show me that life is short, that every moment needs to be lived for his glory. I am not sure what that really looks like, but I do not want to miss it! How do I not miss

it? I pray for progress in healing and really want that. I do not think that is wrong as I have learned from Psalm 28:1–2:

Psalm 28:1–2 To you I call, O Lord my Rock; do not turn a deaf ear to me. For if you remain silent, I will be like those who have gone down to the pit. Hear my cry for mercy as I call to you for help, as I lift up my hands toward your Most Holy Place.

Facet #2: My cancer is from and is designed by God for my benefit and for the benefit of others [Job 2:1–10; 42:11]. This is a beautiful design! When I hold the diamond up to the light, I see deeply into my life and the lives of others, the many beneficiaries of this! Cut and designed for our good . . . please do not let me miss this, Lord! Please do not let others miss this, Lord! . . . Please help me to seek your beauty in all this, Lord! Let me see the Master Jeweler's work in this facet.

As I continue to look at the cut of this beautiful diamond, I see its magnificence in a more opulent way. . . . O the beauty and splendor of it all! But the beauty is not really the diamond itself, but in the Master Jeweler as He displays His beauty. What a strange dichotomy I see—the beauty of the Lord displayed in the beauty of the disease . . . for my good, but ultimately for His glory! . . . Lord, please continue to reveal your glory through my cancer. Let me and others be astounded by it as you work through it! Amen.

Larry and Alana Parrish

The Parrishes are also members of our church. On August 15, 2012, their son Andy was hit by a car going sixty-nine miles per hour. His head struck the windshield. Somehow he survived the accident but suffered massive head trauma. The surgeons at Duke Hospital said that, if he lived, the journey ahead would be a marathon, not a sprint. Watching Larry and Alana care for their dear son over the course of that marathon has changed my life. His needs are relentless: he has a trach tube through which he breathes, and it needs to be regularly suctioned out to keep him from suffocating; he is nonverbal; he cannot walk or sit alone and has to be lifted out of bed daily for physical therapy; he has to be fed and cared for in countless ways I will not describe here.

Larry's and Alana's lives have been permanently altered by this grueling regimen. I remember thinking privately once, much to my later shame, "It would have been so much easier for them if Andy had died in the street. Andy would have gone to heaven, and they could have grieved and gone on with their lives." One day, Larry was pleasantly talking to me as he stroked Andy's hair and talked about how unspeakably grateful he is to God for sparing Andy's life. He and Alana delight in caring for their son; they are glad they still get to look on his face in the land of the living. Feeding him and caring for him is a small price to pay for the indescribable gift of having him here to love. At that time I was preaching through Galatians 2, and a verse came alive as I watched Larry's evident pleasure in serving Andy: "I have been crucified with Christ, and I no longer live, but Christ lives in me" (v. 20 CSB). *I no longer live.*

If I were to call Larry or Alana today and ask what their plans are, they would answer, "Serving Christ by taking care of Andy." I am still learning what "I no longer live" means—forsaking my own plans and pleasures so I can love Jesus by loving others. Their supernatural contentment has been one of the most powerful and convicting living lessons of my life.

The Pain and Tears Are Real

In all of this, we should never forget that the pain and tears are real. God is gracious and compassionate, and he hears the cries of his people (Exod. 2:25; 3:7). God catches our tears in a bottle (Ps. 56:8). As I reread the story of Joseph and saw the emotion that poured from the main characters, I realized again the human cost of the plans of God. When Jacob received Joseph's blood-soaked ornate robe from his lying, murderous sons, he said through anguished tears, "'It is my son's robe. . . . A vicious animal has devoured him! Joseph has been torn to pieces!' Then Jacob tore his clothes, put sackcloth around his waist, and mourned for his son many days. All his sons and daughters tried to comfort him, but he refused to be comforted. 'No,' he said. 'I will go down to Sheol to my son, mourning.' And his father wept for him" (Gen. 37:33–35 CSB).

Jacob mourned for Joseph day after day for years. He never forgot. He never got over it. He was still talking about it years later when Joseph's brothers brought him news that Joseph was alive in Egypt. At that time, God spoke to Jacob in a vision at night, saying that he should go down to Egypt and that God would bring him back to the promised land. Then he said these poignant words: "Joseph's hand shall close your eyes" (Gen. 46:4). God allowed his beloved son Jacob to suffer all those years in the mistaken grief of thinking that Joseph was dead, having been torn to pieces by wild animals. All those tears. All that sorrow. God's awesome plans involved murderous jealousy, cold-hearted lying, and years of grief based on a faulty conception of reality.

Meanwhile, Joseph's pains were every bit as real as those of his father. We see it all come to a head with the overpowering emotion Joseph showed when he finally saw his brother Benjamin. Barely able to control himself, he said, "May God be gracious to you, my son" (Gen. 43:29 NASB). Then "Joseph hurried out because he was overcome with emotion for his brother, and he was about to weep. He went into an inner room and wept there" (v. 30 CSB). When he then orchestrated a final test for his brothers and framed Benjamin for a theft he didn't commit, Judah pleaded with Joseph on behalf of his father that he be allowed to take Benjamin's place (Gen. 44).[14] At that point, Joseph could not control his emotions any longer. He cried out to his brothers, "I am Joseph! Is my father still alive?" (45:3). He wept so loudly that Pharaoh and all his household heard it. That is the human cost of the marvelous plan of God.

I believe this is precisely why Jesus wept before raising Lazarus from the dead (John 11:35). It was out of compassion for the grief and agony that the "last enemy," death (1 Cor. 15:26), would cause for centuries. He feels very deeply the agony of that rending loss. He knows that at millions of funerals over the centuries, his people weep at the loss of a loved one, and he will not step in at that moment to turn wailing into dancing. Christ's tears are the perfect display of the compassion of our heavenly Father, "for he does not enjoy bringing affliction or suffering on mankind" (Lam. 3:33 CSB). So while Christian contentment is a sweet, inward, quiet, gracious frame of spirit that freely submits to and delights in God's wise and fatherly disposal in the midst of soul-piercing loss, God is deeply moved and troubled by the emotions loss will cause. He knows his plan is not achieved for free. It cost his Son everything he had; he knows it will cost you too.

Seven Prayerful Meditations to Help Sufferers Conquer

I close with a brief summary of seven prayerful meditations that I hope will help you conquer Satan and any deeply rooted sin.

God, You Are My Mighty King, and I Am Your Humble Servant

Reflect deeply on God as the exalted King of the Universe. "All the inhabitants of the earth are counted as nothing, and he does what he wants with the army of heaven and the inhabitants of the earth. There is no one who can block his hand or say to him, 'What have you done?'" (Dan. 4:35 CSB). Include yourself in that, saying, "Almighty God, you sit enthroned high above the circle of the earth, and all nations are as nothing to you. I am just one person, small compared even to mighty nations. Lord, you knit me together in my mother's womb, and everything I am or own or love is yours to do with as you please. I humble myself before you and present myself to you as your servant. Do whatever you want with me."

God, You Are My Tender and Compassionate Father

It is also true that God is your adoptive heavenly Father and that his love for you is vastly greater than the love any sinful human father has for his children (Luke 11:13). Remind yourself that the measure of God's love for you is the gift of his only begotten Son, poured out on the cross. "He who did not spare his own Son but gave him up for us all, how will he not also with him graciously give us all things?" (Rom. 8:32). Any other earthly blessing is infinitely less costly to the Father. If he is therefore withholding a blessing, it's not because he doesn't love you or doesn't have the power to give it. Rather, he is wise and loving and is working out a vast plan for the final salvation of all his elect. Meanwhile, your heavenly Father is tender toward you and cares deeply about the pain you are enduring. Pour out your heart to him! Say, "My Father, I am really suffering now. The things you have willed to do in my life are hurting me deeply. I know you care for me infinitely more than I care for myself. Please comfort me, Abba, Father. Pour out your love into my heart through the Holy Spirit. Heal my soul, O Lord, because this hurts!"

God, You Are My Very Great and Eternal Treasure

It is true that God is our eternal treasure. He is our very great reward (Gen. 15:1), our heavenly inheritance (Eph. 1:14). Psalm 73 says it perfectly, and our words can never improve this inspired prayer. So pray it now to God:

> When I became embittered
> and my innermost being was wounded,
> I was stupid and didn't understand;
> I was an unthinking animal toward you.
> Yet I am always with you;
> you hold my right hand.
> You guide me with your counsel,
> and afterward you will take me up in glory.
> Who do I have in heaven but you?
> And I desire nothing on earth but you.

151

My flesh and my heart may fail,
but God is the strength of my heart,
my portion forever. (vv. 21–26 CSB)

God, I Must Kiss the Rod and Cover My Mouth

It is also true that we are deeply idolatrous, mercenary, just like Gomer, whose prostituting heart had to be purchased by her patient, grieving husband (Hosea 3:2–3). We understand that God had to lower himself to wean us bit by bit from the earthly passions that have so captured our eyes and our hearts. He had to, in a sense, humble himself to keep loving us and wooing us back from the worldly loves that have filled up the affections that were meant for him.[15]

It takes this kind of suffering to cause us to realize earlier than our deathbeds that all things in life are temporary. Realize that a part of the pain you are suffering is the loving rod of chastisement from a heavenly Father who will not allow idols to control your heart. There is nothing God can ever do in this world that is more terrifying than to give a sinner over to his sins (Rom. 1:24, 26, 28). This he will never do to any of his children. Instead, he will lovingly and powerfully work in your heart, chastising you to wean you from idols until you love him purely. Hebrews 12:6 says, "The Lord disciplines the one he loves, and chastises every son he receives."

So kiss the rod. Thank God he is so powerfully dealing with you, rather than giving you over to your sins. But also be prepared to put your hand over your mouth, for there is still more corruption deep inside, and Satan is prepared to tempt you to speak hard words against God. Understand: I am not saying that each moment of our suffering is a direct result of specific sin. Not at all. So pray, "Father, I know you have brought this affliction into my life because there is deeply rooted sin in my inner nature. My heart is a wandering heart, and I know I don't love you as I should. Please forgive me for my idols, for all of the earthly gifts I have become addicted to. Wean me from earth. I delight in the ultimate joy that is set before me, and I trust in you. Set a guard over the door of my mouth, Lord. Help me not to sin by charging you with wrongdoing."

Jesus, You Are with Me as I Walk through the Fire

Jesus is called "Immanuel," meaning "God with us" (Matt. 1:23). Jesus has promised plainly, "I will never leave you nor forsake you" (Heb. 13:5). By the Spirit, Jesus is present with you right now, and even in the midst of the greatest suffering you have ever endured.

Shadrach, Meshach, and Abednego, when they were cast into the fiery furnace, were not alone; one like the Son of God was with them in the midst of their trial (Dan. 3:25). Jesus somehow protected them from the heat, and when they came out, their clothes and hair were not even singed, and there was not even the smell of fire on them (v. 27). This was the physical and miraculous fulfillment of the spiritual promise made to all God's children: "When you pass through the waters, I will be with you; and through the rivers, they will not overflow you. When you walk through the fire, you will not be scorched, nor will the flame burn you" (Isa. 43:2 NASB).

Nothing the Father brings you through will ever destroy you. Christ is with you and will guarantee that the fire of the trial will only purify your soul. So pray, "Jesus, you are Immanuel, God with me. You have chosen to make me pass through this fiery trial. Be with me now as you were with Shadrach, Meshach, and Abednego centuries ago. Stand at my side and give me strength as you did when Paul was on trial before Caesar. Let me be very conscious of your presence now; I feel I need you more now than I have ever needed you before. Pray for me to the Father that my faith will not fail, as you prayed for Peter."

God, You Are Fitting Me for Heaven

In the end, we don't need to wonder, "Why, O Lord?"; for all trials and afflictions are brought into our lives so that God may perfect us through endurance (James 1:2–4). Paul says plainly that "this light momentary affliction is preparing for us an eternal weight of glory beyond all comparison" (2 Cor. 4:17).

Light. Momentary. It will be over like a morning mist that quickly passes away. And it is essential to prepare us for heavenly glory. All trials are essential to our sanctification, and the more painful and massive the suffering, the more significant must be the progress God makes in your soul. So freely submit to and delight in God's wise and fatherly work of salvation in your life.

Pray, "Heavenly Father, you are preparing me for a glory that infinitely outweighs anything I am going through now. I know that without afflictions, I cannot grow in Christlikeness. Without suffering, I cannot love you or serve you in any way that is genuine and meaningful. I gladly submit to the work you are doing in me. I yearn for heaven, when all of my brothers and sisters in Christ will stand in your glory and look back on the light and momentary work you did in them."

God, You Have Put Me on a Lampstand

Finally, it is vital to recognize that our tears—even our blood—may well be "seed for the church." God considers us sheep for the slaughter as he did his own Son (Rom. 8:36; Rev. 5:6, 9). We should be willing to suffer great things for the advance of the gospel. Many missionaries buried their spouses, multiple children, and all their earthly hopes to see unreached people come to faith in Christ.

The world watches as we suffer. Be mindful of that. Seek to do the work of the circumstance and discover what good works God has prepared in advance for you to walk in (Eph. 2:10). Suffer well; suffer full of hope. Seek to witness to lost medical professionals, lost funeral home workers, lost co-workers who come to commiserate with you and offer condolences. Put hope on display. Also be mindful that your children are watching you, as are other Christians. You have a responsibility to suffer well in front of them too, so that they may be strengthened by your trial.

Seek strength from the Lord in prayer. Say, "Father, I want to shine in a dark place. You have crafted this intense suffering as a lampstand for me, and you want me to give light to everyone in the house. Give me supernatural strength to suffer well, so that I can be an instrument of the gospel in everyone who watches me. Fill me with hope, that I may minister hope to them." In this way, we will grow in our delight in God's plan for our lives and will be more and more humbly submissive to him directing us in it.

ten

CONTENTMENT
IN PROSPERITY

Jeremiah Burroughs did not think it necessary to write this chapter. He concluded his entire work with these words: "These are afflictive times, and in such times as these, there are few that have such an abundance that they need to be much taught in the lesson of how to abound."[1]

But that is far from our case! Never in the history of the church of Jesus Christ have so many of his disciples been so wealthy. For the most part, Christians in world history have been poor and downtrodden, not wealthy and powerful. The apostle Paul made this plain from the beginning of the church in Corinth: "Not many of you were wise according to worldly standards, not many were powerful, not many were of noble birth" (1 Cor. 1:26). As Christianity spread throughout the Roman Empire, the gospel found powerful success among slaves more than any other level of Roman society. That has continued throughout the centuries all over the world. In India, the single largest bloc of Christians comes from the Dalit ("untouchable") caste, the lowest caste in Indian society.[2] The overwhelming majority of Christians in the world live in abject poverty. But I believe most people who will read this book are in an entirely different category.

In the wake of the Reformation, many in the European nations and America grew stunningly prosperous while maintaining a strong Christian piety. In the New World, the "Protestant work ethic" combined with remarkable providential blessings to produce staggering levels of wealth such as most Christians around the world could scarcely dream of. But with that wealth came a very high cost in their spiritual lives. New England Puritan leader Cotton Mather put it this way: "Religion begat prosperity and the daughter devoured the mother."[3]

American evangelicals of the twenty-first century are the wealthiest Christians in the history of the church. According to one study, evangelicals worldwide collectively made $7 trillion in income for that year.[4] The Christian income in America represents nearly half of the world's total Christian income.[5] That is a massively weighty responsibility for American Christians. Jesus said, "Everyone to whom much was given, of him much will be required" (Luke 12:48). This amazing amount of wealth is a doorway of opportunity for American Christians to alleviate physical suffering in this world and spiritual suffering in eternity. But wealth is also a powerful temptation toward the corruption of our souls. Christian contentment—the ability to maintain a godly demeanor in free and delighted submission under God's fatherly hand—is essential for rich American Christians to use their money wisely and not be polluted by it.

Evidence of Sinful Spending Habits

The statistics are not promising for the true heart condition of many American Christians. The Barna Group reported that in the year 2000, the mean per capita donation by Americans to churches was $649. Seventeen percent of Christians claim to tithe, but only six percent actually do. An amazing 23 percent of Christians gave literally *nothing* in 2000.[6] On what are all those American Christian dollars being spent? What account will those American Christian consumers give to Christ on Judgment Day?

I am particularly interested in money given to mission agencies that are targeting unreached people groups (UPGs). A people group is a group of human individuals identified by a common language and culture and a shared self-identity. Joshua Project designates it as an "unreached" people group if "there is no indigenous community of believing Christians with adequate numbers and resources to evangelize this people group without outside assistance."[7] Of the already too little money given to charitable causes by wealthy American Christians, only a very small percentage is given to foreign missions. Of that very small percentage, only a very small percentage is given to UPGs.

This is the total picture according to one study:

Annual income of all Christians worldwide: $42 trillion

Annual income of evangelical Christians worldwide: $7 trillion

Amount given to any Christian cause: $700 billion
(that's also the amount Americans spend annually on Christmas)

Amount given to missions: $45 billion

(that's how much Americans spend on dieting programs)

Of all the money given to Christian causes:

$677 billion (96.8%) is spent on local church ministries

$20.3 billion (2.9%) is spent on "home missions" in the giver's country

$2.1 billion (0.3%) is spent on already reached non-Christian nations (not UPGs)

$450 million (0.06%) is spent on UPGs[8]

To put this in perspective, for every $100,000 that Christians make, $1 goes to reaching people who have never heard of Christ. Jesus said, "This gospel of the kingdom will be proclaimed throughout the whole word as a testimony to all nations, and then the end will come" (Matt. 24:14). This is the very task that Jesus left us on earth to do. Not everyone is called on to be a cross-cultural missionary, but every Christian is called on to be sacrificially involved in the spread of the gospel to the ends of the earth. As William Carey, the so-called father of modern missions, said to a congregation from which he was soliciting aid for his mission to India, "I will go down into the dark hole of heathenism, but you must hold the ropes for me."[9] Carey was calling on Christians who were not getting on the boat with him to India to support him continually through their money, prayers, and other forms of encouragement. For the vast majority of us who are not gifted and called to become career missionaries, we are going to be involved in the spread of the gospel to UPGs by "holding the ropes" for those who do go, and that means significant sacrifices.

I could do this same kind of analysis concerning the physical needs of poor people in America and around the world, but I've made the point. On Judgment Day, we will have to give an account for every careless word we have spoken (Matt. 12:36) and every careless dollar we have spent. When we look at all the nonessential ways we spend the money we have been provided by God, we will have ample grounds for repentance: cable TV, Netflix, smartphone data packages, dining out, expensive vacations, luxury items (clothes, cars, watches, electronics), and much more.

The questions before us are these: (1) Have we sinfully spent money on ourselves that God intended us to give away? (2) What heart condition has caused this choice? (3) What is the remedy for the way we've used our money?

Concerning the remedy, I want to assert that part of the problem with idolatrous materialism is that we haven't learned the secret of being content—freely submitting to God's wise, fatherly choices for our lives while being well fed and living in plenty. God desires wealthy Christians to learn contentment as pipelines of blessing to others while giving much of their abundant wealth away. Christian contentment that doesn't learn how to be independent of material blessings while surrounded by abundant prosperity will not be much use to those of us who live lavishly blessed lives here in America.

Paul Learned the Secret of Contentment in Prosperity

When I speak to people about the challenges of living out a clear display of Christian contentment, people's minds rightly gravitate to times of suffering. The greatest challenges we will ever face to a "sweet, inward, quiet, gracious frame of spirit" are when our world seems to be falling apart, when we look to the heavens as Job did and cry out in pain to God.

But when everything is going well, it seems at least on the surface that contentment is a given. C. S. Lewis wrote, "Everyone feels benevolent if nothing happens to be annoying him at the moment."[10] It's very easy to feel satisfied and at peace with the universe when the five senses are sated and there are no storm clouds on the horizon. That kind of "contentment" is what the pagans seek continually and run after with all their might. When prosperous circumstances surround you, when you have experienced the blessings of God in everything you have put your hand to, when God has "put a hedge" around you and everything you possess (Job 1:10), the happiness you feel in your heart and display on your face will hardly appear to be supernatural to an unbeliever.

However, appearances can be deceiving. The heavenly commandment of being content is binding as much in prosperity as it is when we are crushed by circumstances. This is evident from Paul's statement in Philippians 4:10–13 that was the scriptural launching for our meditations on Christian contentment. What caused Paul to bring up the topic was a good thing, a moment of prosperity—they had sent money to meet his needs. You can picture Epaphroditus, their messenger, sitting there in the prison cell with Paul, a bag full of silver coins between them. His words are full of the rich delight that filled his heart: "I rejoiced in the Lord greatly," he says (v. 10). But, ever the teacher of the gospel, he wanted to explain his joy so they wouldn't misunderstand it. "Obviously you're full of joy, Paul. You have a money bag on the ground at your feet! Who wouldn't be happy with that?!"

Paul then gives his statement on Christian contentment, and times of richness and prosperity are most definitely involved: "Not that I am speaking of being in need, for I have learned in whatever situation I am to be content. I know how to be brought low, and *I know how to abound*. In any and every circumstance, I have learned the secret of facing *plenty* and hunger, *abundance* and need. I can do all things through him who strengthens me" (Phil. 4:11–13).

Paul considered properly facing times of abundance and plenty as part of the secret.

What times of abundance did Paul experience in his Christian life? Scripture contains far more evidence of times of suffering and deprivation than times of abundance. As Christ told Ananias, "I will show him how much he must suffer for the sake of my name" (Acts 9:16). But we can easily imagine that Paul ate very well and had rich accommodations in the house of Lydia, the first convert to Christ in Philippi and a dealer in purple goods. Purple articles were a symbol of lavish wealth, so most likely Lydia was wealthy, and she invited Paul and his companions to stay at her home while they ministered in Philippi (16:5).

Paul knew how to live in such luxuriant surroundings without being corrupted.

We could extend the same to the house of Publius, the "chief man of the island" of Malta where Paul was shipwrecked. As we saw earlier, Publius warmly extended hospitality to Paul and his companions (Acts 28:7). What could that mean other than offering the finest food and drink he had, and accommodations in a luxurious home?

Paul did not advocate the lifestyle of an ascetic. He rejected the antiphysical philosophy of false teachers who said that godliness comes from extreme self-discipline in the physical world: "Do not handle, Do not taste, Do not touch" (Col. 2:21). When the time came to sit down at a banquet table, he could enjoy the food and drink with a gracious spirit, thankful both to the Lord who gave such delights and to the human host or hostess who provided them.

But there was a secret to Paul's contentment even at that moment. Remember that the word he used for content was "self-sufficient"—not *needing* that feast, not addicted to wine or good times. He told the Corinthians, "I discipline my body and bring it under strict control, so that after preaching to others, I myself will not be disqualified" (1 Cor. 9:27 CSB). He watched his habits and tendencies constantly, because he knew how addictive the "good life" can be. He was willing to sit and enjoy the delicacies of the banquet table, but he never wanted to become enslaved by his tastes (6:12).

The book of Proverbs instructs everyone about earthly pleasures by giving us the rule book on honey. Physical honey is a sweet, golden substance made by bees that brings delight to the tongue. But it is also a metaphor for the good things of life. God tells us, "My son, eat honey, for it is good, and the drippings of the honeycomb are sweet to your taste" (Prov. 24:13). In other words, "I designed the sweetness of honey and the corresponding taste buds on your tongue to give you pleasure. Enjoy!" But having said that, he gives three times as many warnings about honey:

- "If you have found honey, eat only enough for you, lest you have your fill of it and vomit it" (25:16). In other words, don't overindulge in the good things of life.

- "It is not good to eat much honey, nor is it glorious to seek one's own glory" (v. 27). Again, don't overindulge, and don't make the pursuit of personal "honey" your focus in life.
- "One who is full loathes honey, but to one who is hungry everything bitter is sweet" (27:7). A great danger of a life full of pleasure is that, after a while, we will lose the taste of all the good things because we have indulged in them so much that nothing satisfies us anymore.

A content man or woman knows when to push away from the banquet table. For an evening, they enjoy the delicacies set before them, but they are not enslaved by them. Their true happiness comes in Christ, and they have no need to overeat or become affected by wine.

We wealthy American Christians are surrounded at every moment with sweet honey dripping from the comb. No generation of Christians in history has been so tempted to swim in an Olympic-size pool of honey, drowning ourselves in earthly pleasures. We make more money than we need for basic necessities (food, clothing, shelter), and the nearest malls and online shopping sites beckon. Christian contentment frees us from the extremes of both overindulgence and asceticism.

The Corrupt Prosperity Gospel: 1 Timothy 6:3–10

The prosperous West has given rise in these latter days to a heresy that has been exported from America to the distant corners of the earth: the prosperity gospel. "This false gospel teaches that God wants to fulfill our every desire for health, wealth, and happiness, and all it takes is sufficient faith. The preachers of prosperity tout their own opulent lifestyles as proof of their message: God wants his children to have it all."[11] Of the largest two hundred sixty churches in the United States, fifty promote the prosperity gospel.[12] The core of the prosperity gospel is idolatry: a strong belief that ultimate blessedness comes from created things. And this, of course, feeds a continual greediness that is the essence of discontentment. This is *not* the secret of Christian contentment that Paul taught and lived.

Paul refuted the same false teaching in 1 Timothy 6:3–10. In that passage, Paul warns Timothy about false teachers who teach that "godliness is a way to material gain" (v. 5 CSB). This is exactly what we see in the lifestyle of these prosperity teachers who live in lavish mansions, fly in private jets, and drive expensive sports cars. But, says Paul, "godliness with contentment is great gain" (v. 6 CSB). He uses the same basic Greek word for contentment as in Philippians 4:11—"self-sufficiency," the blessed state of independence from all created things.

To be genuinely godly and to be independent from addiction to material possessions is the richest you can be in this world. To reach the point where our only needs are basic physical necessities—food, clothing, and shelter—and we are truly satisfied with that, that is true wealth (1 Tim. 6:8).

Christian contentment can enable someone to be amazingly generous with the surplus he has earned. As Paul says in 2 Corinthians 8:15, "Whoever gathered much had nothing left over, and whoever gathered little had no lack." Because he had no family and lived in a noninflationary age, John

Wesley was able to live his whole life on the same income he made his first year of ministry. His income increased every year his entire life, but he never increased his personal expenses. He just gave away everything above a certain amount. Randy Alcorn cites Wesley's example, suggesting that God may well give us extra money (in a raise, a bonus, an inheritance, a refund, etc.) in order to increase not our standard of *living* but our standard of *giving*.[13] Christian contentment frees the person who gathers much from holding on to it and allows them instead to give it away to alleviate earthly suffering and spread the gospel.

Sound Investment Advice for Prosperous Christians: First Timothy 6:17–19

In that same chapter, Paul goes on to give excellent advice for us prosperous Christians. Everyone who is rich with earthly blessings should memorize 1 Timothy 6:17–19 and continually evaluate whether he or she is being obedient to this clear teaching: "As for the rich in this present age, charge them not to be haughty, nor to set their hopes on the uncertainty of riches, but on God, who richly provides us with everything to enjoy. They are to do good, to be rich in good works, to be generous and ready to share, thus storing up treasure for themselves as a good foundation for the future, so that they may take hold of that which is truly life" (1 Tim. 6:17–19).

Contentment starts with humility. Wealth can make us arrogant, as though we are somehow intrinsically superior to the poor: smarter, harder working, more disciplined. It's even worse if we add spiritual superiority to that list: "I am wealthy because I am holier than they are. God is blessing my godliness with earthly success." Paul wants rich Christians to begin with humility, to not be haughty or arrogant toward their poorer Christian brothers and sisters.

Second, Paul warns prosperous Christians not to set their hopes on material wealth, because it is so fleeting (1 Tim. 6:17). "When your eyes light on wealth, it is gone, for suddenly it sprouts wings, flying like an eagle toward heaven" (Prov. 23:5).

Money can turn hearts away from faith in Christ and turn them toward faith in money. In 1856, Charles Spurgeon was raising money for the Metropolitan Tabernacle in London, the massive church building in which he would preach for the rest of his life to thousands of people. A wealthy benefactor approached Spurgeon privately and promised him twenty thousand pounds for the completion of the project if the funds should fail to come in by the needed time. A friend who was aware of the secret offer said to Spurgeon cheerfully, "Isn't it easier to trust God for the rest of the money now?" Spurgeon answered, "Not at all; it's easier to trust the twenty thousand pounds!"[14]

Third, instead of this false trust, Christians with wealth should continue to trust in God, who richly provides us with everything we enjoy in life (1 Tim. 6:17). Wealthy people can enjoy some of the earthly blessings given them by God. But they must not allow these temporary blessings to steal their hearts away from Christ. As they enjoy higher levels of earthly blessing than millions of their brothers and sisters in Christ are experiencing, they should realize that God loves those poor children of his as much as he loves them. During the Great Reversal of Judgment Day, the last shall come to the front as first.

Fourth, rich Christians should do good works to build the kingdom (1 Tim. 6:18). Because of their extreme blessings, they should be able to partner with other wealthy Christians to fund major projects that need to be done—buildings that need to be built, disaster relief that will aid the devastated, thousands of missionaries that need to be supported. Those with wealth can bear a huge load of these material needs. By doing this they will store up treasure in heaven (v. 19). They will show their lives were never about the money.

As an example, look at R. G. LeTourneau, whose company designed and built massive earth-moving equipment. He was fabulously wealthy and freely generous. He gave away 90 percent of all his company's profits to Christian work. The money came in faster than he could give it away. He said, "I shovel it out, and God shovels it back. But God has a bigger shovel."[15] This is an example of what Paul was commanding rich Christians to do with their money.

If prosperous Christians will follow these four steps, Paul says they will escape the corruptions of money and will be eternally wealthy in heaven. Christian contentment will enable them to take their abundant prosperity and to humbly kneel with a sweet, quiet, inward, gracious frame of spirit, acknowledging that everything they own belongs to the heavenly Father and that he means them to be a pipeline of his blessings to others. With that content spirit they will continually send their money quickly[16] on its way into needy hands and God's record books. At Judgment Day they too will receive their reward.

PART 4

KEEPING
CONTENT

eleven

CONTENTMENT
IS NOT COMPLACENCY

Christianity is a relentless force, like a thundering waterfall of power and beauty that roars that God should be glorified to every corner of his creation. Christianity exists in a universe presently at war, a divided creation split apart by evil. The devil led the way in the revolt against a holy God, and we humans joined in his rebellion. The resulting curse has made all of creation groan under the chains of bondage to decay. Our own souls cry out against our sinfulness: "What a wretched man I am! Who will rescue me from this body of death?" (Rom. 7:24 CSB).

In the middle of such high stakes, a default to the status quo is a default to the devil. Allowing any evil at all in God's universe is intolerable. The more someone grows in Christ, the more passionate will be their commitment to see God's will done on earth. "Our God is a consuming fire"

(Heb. 12:29), and his Holy Spirit works to kindle the same holy flame in the hearts of his people.

How then do peace, joy, and Christian contentment co-exist with the relentless force and drive and power of Christianity? It seems unfitting for a Christian ever to relax, to be at peace, quiet, resting under God's mighty hand.

This question came to my attention when I was teaching Christian contentment to a group of Wycliffe Bible translators in Cameroon. One of them pulled me aside and said, "Honestly, I never thought that contentment was something we should strive for in a lost and dying world." The more we talked and the more I came to understand his passion to see the Scriptures translated into a language that had never had the Word of God before, I saw how vital it was for me to clarify the difference between contentment and complacency.

Satan's Numbing Sting

Twice in the famous works of J. R. R. Tolkien, characters in the story are attacked by evil spiders. The first occurs in *The Hobbit* when the hero, Bilbo, rescues his companions, a band of dwarves, from a nest of gigantic spiders. The dwarves have been stung, paralyzed, and wrapped up in sticky webs, left hanging in something like cocoons. Bilbo uses his sword, his courage, his clever schemes, and the ring, which makes him invisible, to kill many of the spiders and lead the rest away. While they are gone, he cuts the dwarves free from their webbed prisons and wakes them from the effects of the toxins in their bloodstreams. The same kind of incident occurs in *The Lord of the Rings* when a giant spider, Shelob, stings Frodo, paralyzes him, and wraps him—he is almost dead. His faithful companion Sam Gamgee does not at first understand that his master is still alive. Sam realizes Frodo's true condition just in time to rescue him.

This image pictures what I mean by "complacency," a lazy, sluggish, poisoned approach to life that mimics death by accepting Satan's evil status quo. It has stayed in my mind as I consider Paul's powerful assessment of unbelievers in Satan's dark kingdom: "And you were dead in the trespasses and sins in which you once walked, following the course of this world, following the prince of the power of the air, the spirit that is now at work in the sons of disobedience—among whom we all once lived in the passions of our flesh, carrying out the desires of the body and the mind, and were by nature children of wrath, like the rest of mankind" (Eph. 2:1–3).

Essentially, this text tells us that the lost are dead while they live, walking under the continual power of Satan's invisible evil influence. The world system Satan sets up pollutes their minds with temptation to sin, and demons secretly push these lusts deeper and deeper into their souls. They do not realize that they are "harassed and helpless, like sheep without a shepherd" (Matt. 9:36)—or like Frodo and the dwarves.

My focus here is on the residual effects of the spiders' poison in our spiritual bloodstream. When we are raised from the dead spiritually by the power of Christ through the gospel (Eph. 2:5), we are made new creatures in Christ (2 Cor. 5:17) and given the mind of Christ (1 Cor. 2:16). We are set free from Satan's dark dominion and transferred forever into the kingdom of the Son of God (Col. 1:13). Yet for all of that, we still have sin living within us, twisting our minds and slanting our affections away from the holy things of God (Rom. 7:21–23).

It's as though we still have the sluggishness and paralysis that Satan's poisonous sting has produced. We can look at spiritually tragic situations and barely respond; we can see significant sin patterns in ourselves and others and not be moved; we can walk by homeless people in large cities and barely glance their way. Clearly something is wrong, even still, with our hearts. Christian contentment does not excuse these dead responses. Christian contentment is *not* complacency!

Zeal for Personal Holiness

The sun burns continually in the sky, lighting and heating the world with an almost incalculable energy. Scientists tell us that within the span of one second, the sun generates enough energy to fuel the earth's human industries for half a million years. The surface of the sun burns at 10,000 degrees Fahrenheit. The core burns at an almost unimaginable 27 million degrees! Yet this raging ball of nuclear fire is sustained every moment by Almighty God. And not just this one star, but every star in the universe: "Look up and see! Who created these? He brings out the stars by number; he calls all of them by name. Because of his great power and strength, not one of them is missing" (Isa. 40:26 CSB). These staggering truths help me to understand what it means when Scripture says that our God is a consuming fire, that "God is light, and in him is no darkness at all" (1 John 1:5). This all-consuming fire is the source of every Christian's passion for holiness, not just for ourselves but for all of our brothers and sisters in Christ.

Zeal for holiness drives our sanctification; laziness and sinful complacency fight it every step of the way. The apostle Paul

clearly displayed in his own life a personal drive for total con-
formity to Christ. He saw on the road to Damascus a portion
of the glory of the resurrected Christ, and it kindled in him
a relentless desire to know Christ and be conformed to him.
Paul yearned to see the indwelling sin in his life obliter-
ated. His personal life was a relentless quest to be perfect
as Christ is perfect: "Not that I have already obtained it or
have already become perfect, but *I press on* so that I may
lay hold of that for which also I was laid hold of by Christ
Jesus. Brethren, I do not regard myself as having laid hold
of it yet; but one thing I do: forgetting what lies behind and
reaching forward to what lies ahead, *I press on* toward the
goal for the prize of the upward call of God in Christ Jesus"
(Phil. 3:12–14 NASB).

Paul's "pressing on" after Christlike perfection was one
of the two central drives of his life. He took painful steps
every single day to be sure he was pressing after holiness
with relentless zeal. He wrote Romans 7, so he knew very
well the seeds of his own destruction were sown in his flesh,
ready to flare up under the wicked influence of the world and
the devil. He considered himself still the foremost sinner on
earth (1 Tim. 1:15–16), in need of a constant river of grace.
He knew that as the apostle to the gentiles, he had a huge
target on his back, and that Satan would like nothing better
than to disqualify him from ministry through some moral
failure. So he spoke of his relentless vigilance over his soul
with these words: "I run in such a way, as not without aim;
I box in such a way, as not beating the air; but I discipline
my body and make it my slave, so that, after I have preached
to others, I myself will not be disqualified" (1 Cor. 9:26–27
NASB).

Paul's commitment to discipline his body and make it his slave was relentless. He knew that at every moment his flesh would be seeking to seize control of his mind and push him toward shameful sins that would disqualify him for the prize of faithful service to God, and perhaps even heaven itself. This is hardly the language of lazy complacency and spiritual overconfidence. And he was clearly commending this kind of relentless vigilance to every Christian.

Actually, Paul commanded the Ephesian elders to "be on guard for yourselves and for all the flock of which the Holy Spirit has appointed you as overseers" (Acts 20:28 CSB). Rather than lying on a feathery bed of ease, they must have the same sense of sleepless vigilance that the watchmen on the city walls would have had in a time of war. And the elders must include themselves in this same intense watchfulness. As Richard Baxter wrote:

> Take heed to yourselves, lest you live in those sins which you preach against in others, and lest you be guilty of that which daily you condemn. . . . If sin be evil, why do you live in it; if it be not, why do you dissuade men from it? If it be danger-ous, how dare you venture on it? If it be not, why do you tell men so? If God's threatenings be true, why do you not fear them? If they be false, why do you needlessly trouble men with them, and put them into such frights without a cause.[1]

The greatest men and women in the history of the church have been conspicuously passionate about relentlessly pursu-ing personal holiness. In them was no sense of spiritual leth-argy or prideful overconfidence. They mortified sin by the power of the Spirit (Rom. 8:13); they lived "self-controlled, upright, and godly lives" in this present evil age (Titus 2:12). I think about the example of Jonathan Edwards, who made, at age nineteen, an amazing list of spiritual resolutions and sought to fulfill them for the rest of his life with all his might. Listen to several of them:

> 1. Resolved, that I will do whatsoever I think to be most to God's glory, and my own good, profit and pleasure, in the whole of my duration, without any consideration of the time, whether now, or never so many myriads of ages hence. Resolved to do whatever I think to be my duty and most for the good and advantage of mankind in general. Resolved to do this, whatever difficulties I meet with, how many soever, and how great soever. . . .

> 3. Resolved, if ever I shall fall and grow dull, so as to neglect to keep any part of these Resolutions, to repent of all I can remember, when I come to myself again. . . .

> 22. Resolved, to endeavor to obtain for myself as much happiness, in the other world, as I possibly can, with all the power, might, vigor, and vehemence, yea violence, I am capable of, or can bring myself to exert, in any way that can be thought of. . . .

> 56. Resolved, never to give over, nor in the least to slacken, my fight with my corruptions, however unsuccessful I may be.[2]

So also David Brainerd showed a stunning drive toward personal holiness; he took not a single day of rest in pursuing purity of body and soul: "When I really enjoy God, I feel my desires of him the more insatiable, and my thirstings after holiness the more unquenchable. . . . Oh, for holiness! Oh, for more of God in my soul! Oh, this pleasing pain! It makes my soul press after God. . . . Oh, that I might not loiter on my heavenly journey!"[3]

Notice that this is in no way a life of colorless drudgery, of ascetic slavery with no pleasure at all. Rather, it's a life that fits perfectly with true Christian contentment, a life of finding true pleasure in God alone. But there is a relentless zeal, a pace to Brainerd's pursuit, a fear of "loitering" on his heavenly journey. This loitering is what I am here calling complacency, and it is no part of a healthy Christian life.

Beyond this, Christian maturity will also compel us to a deep yearning for the holiness of others and a powerful grief when God's laws are violated. The psalmist lamented bitterly, "My eyes shed streams of tears, because people do not keep your law" (Ps. 119:136). Peter reveals the heart of righteous Lot in seeing the wickedness of Sodom and Gomorrah, saying he was "greatly distressed by the sensual conduct of the wicked, (for as that righteous man lived among them day after day, he was tormenting his righteous soul over their lawless deeds that he saw and heard)" (2 Pet. 2:7–8). Christian contentment is not complacent about the wickedness of our own hearts, of other Christians, or of the world. We "hunger and thirst for righteousness" (Matt. 5:6) and will not be satisfied till we see it fulfilled in Christ's eternal kingdom.

Zeal for the Advance of Christ's Kingdom

In the same way, genuine Christians feel a fire in their hearts that the "earth will be filled with the knowledge of the glory of the LORD as the waters cover the sea" (Hab. 2:14). We cannot be content with the fact that millions of people die every year never having heard the name of Jesus Christ. We must be driven with a relentless passion that we fervently articulate in the pattern of the Lord's Prayer: "O God, my loving heavenly Father, my deepest desire is that your holy name be held in the highest honor by every person on earth, and that your blessed kingdom would come worldwide, and that every human being whom you fashioned for your glory would do your will with the same zeal and diligence with which the angels do it in heaven. Until that comes, O Lord, may I never slacken in my sacrificial service to evangelism and missions" (see Matt. 6:9–10).

The apostle Paul lived out this unquenchable zeal every day after his conversion. No one in church history burned so brightly for the salvation of the lost and the spread of the gospel among those who had never heard God's name or seen his glory (Isa. 66:19). This was the other passion of Paul's life: "But I do not account my life of any value nor as precious to myself, if only I may finish my course and the ministry that I received from the Lord Jesus, to testify to the gospel of the grace of God" (Acts 20:24).

There was no complacency here, no reliance on God's eternal predestination to bring in the elect without human agency. Paul knew very well that all the elect would be saved, but he also knew that without human messengers and great suffering, the perfect redemption worked by Christ would not be applied to a single lost person. "Therefore I endure everything for the sake of the elect, that they also may obtain the salvation that is in Christ Jesus with eternal glory" (2 Tim. 2:10). As Paul reasoned out plainly, "How then will they call on him in whom they have not believed? And how are they to believe in him of whom they have never heard? And how are they to hear without someone preaching? And how are they to preach unless they are sent? As it is written, 'How beautiful are the feet of those who preach the good news!'" (Rom. 10:14–15).

Many Christians in the prosperous West live their lives in self-indulgent luxury and slothful ease while literally billions of people live every day of their lives "without hope and without God in the world" (Eph. 2:12 CSB). Some of the choicest servants in the history of missions have felt a burning passion for the lost and have sounded the clarion call to try to awaken churchgoers out of their sinful sleep.

Hudson Taylor, the great missionary to China, was such a man, and the sight of so many in Scotland sitting comfortably in the pews while teeming millions in the unreached inner regions of China perished apart from Christ burned in his soul: "On Sunday, June 25th, 1865, unable to bear the sight of a congregation of a thousand or more Christian people rejoicing in their own security, while millions were perishing for lack of knowledge, I wandered out on the sands alone, in great spiritual agony; and there the Lord conquered my unbelief, and I surrendered myself to God for this service."[4]

To Taylor, it was simply intolerable that millions of Chinese should go to hell while thousands of Scottish Christians should enjoy their spiritual security. This passion is clearly kindled by the Holy Spirit in the souls of men and women who have been instrumental in the advance of the kingdom of God for twenty centuries. Laziness, lethargy, and self-satisfaction have consistently quenched the Spirit's powerful fire in many local churches and in the hearts of many Christians.

One example of the kind of complacency that the afflu-
ent West has displayed toward missions has come in my own
denomination, the Southern Baptist Convention (SBC). Every
year, the Southern Baptist missions agency collects funds for
missionaries in an offering called the "Lottie Moon Christmas
Offering" (LMCO). In 2014, there were approximately 54,000
Southern Baptist churches, and the total LMCO was $153
million. Ninety-five percent of the offering came from approximately 17,000 of those churches, while the other 37,000
churches gave the other 5 percent. Those 37,000 gave $7.65
million, which amounts to a paltry $200 per church to keep
missionaries on the field winning lost people to Christ. The
next year, the International Mission Board had to cut its missions force by 1,132 people because of lack of funds. It is hard
to imagine that those 37,000 churches couldn't come up with
more than $200 each to keep those laborers in the harvest field.

No Complacency about Hell

The two foremost teachers of Christian contentment—
Christ and Paul—both expressed intense anguish about the
ultimate plight of the damned. The New Testament reveals
most clearly that hell is a place of eternal, conscious torment. Revelation 14:11 says plainly about those condemned
to hell, "The smoke of their torment will go up forever and
ever. There is no rest day or night" (CSB). Jesus taught that
at the time of his judgment of all the earth, he will say to
those condemned, "Depart from me, you who are cursed,
into the eternal fire prepared for the devil and his angels"
(Matt. 25:41 CSB). Because of this, Jesus wept over Jerusalem
(Luke 19:41). The apostle Paul said, "I have great sorrow and

unceasing anguish in my heart" for the lost among the people of Israel (Rom. 9:2). He even went so far as to say he'd be willing to trade his own salvation for theirs (v. 3).

No people in history ever displayed more consistently the principles of Christian contentment—as our definition has said, a sweet, quiet, gracious, inward frame of spirit that freely submitted to and delighted in whatever God the Father ordained. But clearly that was not incompatible with a deep anguish over the eternal plight of the damned in the Lake of Fire and a fervent yearning to save people from that end.

So also many of Christ's choicest servants have been consumed with a passion to free the lost from eternity apart from Christ. Before he went as a missionary to India, William Carey worked as both a shoemaker and a teacher. When he became convinced of the urgency of the plight of the "pagans" in the distant lands who had never heard of Christ, he sought to enflame others with a like passion. He made a shoe-leather globe and held it up before his pupils with great tears, crying aloud, "These are all pagans! Pagans!"[5] It was absolutely intolerable to Carey that they should die without him doing his utmost to bring the gospel to them. We who have sacrificed so little for missions need to hear by faith the cries of the damned long before they are finally condemned, while there is still time for them to be rescued. God forbid that we allow the spiders' poison to numb us to what is soon to come upon so many if they are not converted.

Zeal versus the Complacency of Sodom

This same fiery zeal that God works in our hearts for holiness and missions, he also works regarding the poor and needy.

We live in a world with overwhelming needs, and those needs are pressed to our minds daily by the instantaneous information available through our smartphones. The news feeds are brought right to our hands concerning an earthquake in Haiti, or a hurricane in Mexico, or a tsunami in Indonesia, or a famine in Ethiopia. Christian contentment does not cause us to close our hearts to their cries. We walk through aisle after aisle in our grocery stores, hardly noticing how lavishly stocked the shelves are and seemingly unaware of how unusual that is in world history. I remember returning from my first mission trip to Haiti stunned by the sheer variety of cold cereals available at the large grocery store where I was shopping. Complacency caused by luxury is a very great sin; it is, in fact, the very sin that the prophet Ezekiel exposed concerning Sodom: "Behold, this was the guilt of your sister Sodom: she and her daughters had arrogance, abundant food and careless ease, but she did not help the poor and needy" (Ezek. 16:49 NASB).

Careless ease. Unable to be moved by the plight of the suffering. How easy it is for this to happen to us in our lives of prosperity. We will not be saved by our works, and no amount of charity given to the poor in this world will ever eradicate poverty before the second coming of Christ. However, the Lord is calling us to be more and more sensitive to the cries of the poor, not complacent.

Contentment Actually Protects a Lifetime Zeal

Far from quenching burning zeal for holiness and for the spread of the gospel by a worldly lethargy, genuine Christian contentment protects that fire from being extinguished by adversity. There can be no advance in either personal holiness or evangelism/missions without suffering. If we have not learned the secret of being content while that road gets extremely steep, we will give up. Christian contentment protected Paul's fiery passion for the glory of Christ, and it can protect ours as well. If Adoniram Judson had not found hope in Christ after the overwhelming setbacks of burying a second child and his beloved partner in mission, his wife Nancy, he might well have abandoned the work in Burma just before the thousands he was to convert would have found the Savior.[6] Contentment enabled him to persevere.

twelve

HOW TO ATTAIN AND PROTECT CONTENTMENT

Christian contentment will not come easily. You will need to focus your soul on it, moment after moment, for the rest of your life. Burroughs calls it a skill and an art—as well as a mystery:

> Contentment is possible if you get skill in the art of it; you may attain to it, and it will prove to be not such a difficult thing either, if you but understand the mystery of it. There are many things that men do in their callings, that if a coun tryman comes and sees, he thinks it a mighty hard thing, and that he should never be able to do it. But that is because he does not understand the art of it; there is a twist of the hand by which you may do it with ease.[1]

How long did it take for Michelangelo to develop the skills as a sculptor to make the sinews and vessels in a marble arm look as if they were alive? How long did it take for Antonio

Stradivari in seventeenth-century Italy to develop the skills to make violins that would still be sought, treasured, and played by virtuosos three centuries later? For more normal people, how long does it take to become proficient at a musical instrument or a sport like golf or basketball? This kind of skill simply doesn't come overnight.

Not only does it take remarkable spiritual skill to attain contentment; it also takes immense strength to protect it. You must be a mighty warrior, protecting a treasure of incalculable value. Paul said the secret of being content in any and every circumstance was *strength*: "I can do all things through him who strengthens me" (Phil. 4:13). Picture a walled citadel in the ancient world, anticipating a deadly siege from an invading army. See how diligently they prepare their defenses, how they stock up the fortress with food and water, with weapons and warriors, with defensive engines designed by military geniuses to defeat the besieging foe. Inside the walls of the citadel, helpless citizens will seek protection. But most of the soldiers must have the will to fight. They expect to engage the army, fight, suffer in the fight, and win.

The greatest war story I have ever read was about the Great Siege of Malta in 1565, during a time of terrifying Islamic military expansion toward Europe. Malta, a small, rocky island in the middle of the Mediterranean Sea, was of vast strategic importance. In May of 1565, the ambitious ruler of the powerful Ottoman Empire, Suleiman the Magnificent, sent a massive force to invade the island. Defending Malta were the forces of the Knights Hospitaller, led by Grand Master Jean Parisot de Valette. They numbered only about six thousand, opposing the invading force of forty thousand. At the most dramatic point in the siege, the walls to the fortress were breached by the detonation of a mine. As the debris from the blast was still falling from the air, the Turks charged into the breach. The grand master himself, though seventy years old, leaped down with his sword in his hand and plugged the gap. Following his heroic example, two hundred knights joined him and saved the city.

Such a tale of valor gives us a picture of the determined defense we must wage for consistent contentment. Satan and his demonic forces will assault the citadel of your contentment every moment of your life for the rest of your days on earth. You are called on to "be strong in the Lord and in the strength of his might" (Eph. 6:10). You are called to put on the full armor of God and stand in the evil day, fighting off the schemes of the devil (v. 11). You are facing forces of cosmic evil whose power you can scarcely imagine (v. 12). And if you do not fight, you will be discontent. The demonic forces will defeat you and carry off your treasure.

Picture the most obscure hero in the Bible, a warrior named Shamgar, who took his stand against a Philistine army and killed six hundred soldiers with an oxgoad—little more than a sharpened stick! How did he kill so many with such a weapon? One at a time. So also Satan will come at your contentment in waves, permitted by the Lord, who will not allow you to be tempted beyond what you can bear (1 Cor. 10:13). You must fight his temptations toward discontentment one at a time, relying on the strength of the Lord. "I can do all things through him who strengthens me." David said to the Lord, "He trains my hands for war; my arms can bend a bow of bronze" (Ps. 18:34 CSB). God will teach you to be a skillful warrior and master craftsperson in Christian contentment.

Skilled Christian Warriors Are Not Outliers

Every warrior needs training to reach full maturity. And every skilled craftsperson or artist needs training to perfect his or her craft or artistry. What does it entail? How long does it take?

In his acclaimed book *Outliers*, Malcom Gladwell studied geniuses, leaders in their fields, to ask that very question. He concluded that perfecting one's craft required a combination of natural ability, unusual circumstances, and ten thousand hours of practice.[2] The unusual circumstances gave the genius time to put in those ten thousand hours to hone her craft—unusual circumstances, for example, like parents who drove her early to practices for years or, more specifically, like a computer club on a nearby campus that had skilled programmers to enable a young Bill Gates to hone his interests and his visionary thinking about the world of computers.[3]

The beauty of Christian contentment is that every single day our heavenly Father providentially orchestrates circumstances intended to teach us how to be content "in any and every circumstance." Though it is almost impossible in a normal life to put in ten thousand hours at violin or programming or golf, "any and every circumstance" will most certainly occur every day of our lives. God has planned a curriculum of blessings and trials that can, if used wisely, teach us the secret of contentment in every circumstance we could possibly face. A seemingly random Monday is nothing of the sort. It is a divinely ordained set of lessons he has signed us up to take. Skilled Christian warriors for contentment ought not to be outliers. In Christ, the opportunity and resources are available for us all.

What practical guidance can I give you to become a skillful warrior? The best thing we can do to prepare for a lifetime of growth into Christian contentment is to meditate prayerfully and continually on the weighty themes this book has already covered. Beyond this, I would like to give some final practical guidelines under three headings: "Daily Spiritual Disciplines," "Skillful Soldiering for Contentment," and "Special Projects to Build Contentment."

Daily Spiritual Disciplines

The training manual begins with the importance of a thing called "Today." Hebrews 3–4 opens for us this vital concept based on an extended meditation on Psalm 95:7–8: "Today, if you hear his voice, do not harden your hearts." God established something called "Today" at the very beginning of creation: "There was evening and there was morning, the first day" (Gen. 1:5). The rhythm of night leading to a new day is God's plan for human history, including yours. "His mercies never come to an end; they are new every morning" (Lam. 3:23). So, as each new day starts, there is an opportunity for us to learn the secret of Christian contentment and live it out, for his glory. We cannot obey God yesterday; it is gone into God's perfect record book. We cannot obey God tomorrow, for it has not yet arrived and it never will. When it does come, it will have a new name: Today. The tapestry of our life's history is made up of Todays. And it should start with some basic spiritual disciplines, if we are ever to make progress to maturity in Christian contentment.

New Life in Christ. Dead people can't fight. Before anyone can display skill and strength in the battle for abiding

Christian contentment, he or she must first be raised to spiritual life through faith in Christ (Eph. 2:1–6). If you have trusted in Christ as your Savior, you are ready to fight for contentment. If you are a Christian, you can live out your new life in Christ by the power of the Holy Spirit.

Abide in Christ. Jesus said, "I am the vine; you are the branches. Whoever abides in me and I in him, he it is that bears much fruit, for apart from me you can do nothing" (John 15:5). It is impossible to display the kind of supernatural contentment that this book is about apart from abiding in Christ. The kind of abiding Christ is referring to here is a conscious awareness of vital communion with Christ by the Holy Spirit, by the Word and prayer.

Daily Quiet Time. A daily quiet time is a spiritual necessity, and I would urge it to be first thing in the morning. Jesus showed the way here by getting up a great while before dawn to meet with his Father for prayer (Mark 1:35). Since God's mercies are new every morning (Lam. 3:23), and since we are given a thing called "Today" in which we must hear the Spirit speak by the word and not harden our hearts (Heb. 3:7–8; 4:7), it makes sense to seek God early in the morning before the day has begun. And one of the central goals of our quiet times should be to restore the joy of our salvation to our hearts—to be "happy in the Lord." George Mueller put it this way:

> The first great and primary business to which I ought to attend every day was, to have my soul happy in the Lord. The first thing to be concerned about was not, how much I might serve the Lord, how I might glorify the Lord; but how I might get my soul into a happy state, and how my inner

man might be nourished. For I might seek to set the truth before the unconverted, I might seek to benefit believers, I might seek to relieve the distressed, I might in other ways seek to behave myself as it becomes a child of God in this world; and yet, not being happy in the Lord, and not being nourished and strengthened in my inner man day by day, all this might not be attended to in a right spirit.[4]

For our purposes, the "happy state" of soul and "right spirit" that Mueller sought to achieve every day is Christian contentment. The basic image I have here is that you should reestablish Christian contentment every morning in your quiet time and then fight hard to protect that citadel from the inevitable onslaught of the world, the flesh, and the devil.

Memorize Scripture. In the vine-and-branches teaching, Jesus points to the importance of his words abiding or remaining in us as a necessary condition for producing lasting fruit: "If you remain in me and my words remain in you, ask whatever you want and it will be done for you. My Father is glorified by this: that you produce much fruit and prove to be my disciples" (John 15:7–8 CSB). To have Jesus' words remain in you moment by moment, I would strongly plead with you to memorize Scripture. The "sword of the Spirit" is the Word of God (Eph. 6:17), and by it we can defeat the attacks of Satan on our contentment throughout the day. This is a battle for the mind. Discontent starts with thoughts that get planted in our minds; without the life-giving Word of God to renew our minds, our joy will start to decay. Jesus set the example for us, for when Satan took him to the top of the mountain of testing and showed him all the kingdoms of the world and their glory, Christ refuted him with Scripture (Matt. 4:8–10).[5]

Delight in Christian Contentment. Remind yourself every day how God-exalting and morally excellent Christian contentment is. Reread chapter 7 in this book to go over the various aspects of what makes Christian contentment so excellent in the sight of God. Set this as a goal for your life in general and for the day in particular. Be intensely attracted to contentment at all times.

Disgust for Complaining. Conversely, reestablish your understanding of how repulsive a complaining spirit is in God's sight and of how repulsive it should be to you. Review chapter 8, which discusses the evils and excuses of a complaining spirit, and set your face against this kind of spirit for the whole day.

Search Me, O God. Ask God to reveal any hidden sins in your life based on Psalm 139:23–24. Confess all the sins the Spirit reveals. Especially be ready to confess patterns of sin that are directly related to discontentment: willful sins by which you have violated your conscience. Renounce all of these sins in prayer and accept his full forgiveness based on 1 John 1:9.

Ask for Contentment Right Now. In prayer, ask God to make you content in Christ by the Holy Spirit *right now*. Wait on the Lord to do this, to quiet your soul under his fatherly hand. "Cast all your anxieties on him, because he cares for you" (1 Pet. 5:7).

Pray for Others to Be Content. Lift up the people in your life in prayer, specifically concerning Christian contentment. Ask God to work in their souls, lifting their doubts and fears from their hearts. Extend your prayers out in concentric circles, beginning with your spouse and your family, moving outward to include your church family, then to Christians serving the Lord all over the world.

Be Prepared to Be a Light Set on a Stand. Realize that God has gone before you this very day to prepare good works for you to walk in (Eph. 2:10). God has made you the light of the world and will put you up on a stand (maybe a stand of suffering) to display the hope you have in Christ (Matt. 5:14–16). Be prepared for this in prayer. Ask God to strengthen you to fulfill the role he has chosen for you in his good providence.

Get Ready to Fight All Day Long. Satan will not allow you to remain content in Christ without a strong assault. You must put on the full armor of God and stand your ground (Eph. 6:10–18) in Christian contentment all day long. Ephesians 6 speaks of God's mighty power in you to stand and fight, and that is the essence of Paul's secret: "I can do all things through him who strengthens me" (Phil. 4:13). God will filter Satan's temptations; he will not permit you to be tempted beyond what you can bear but will make a way of escape so you can continue to be content in any and every circumstance (1 Cor. 10:13).

Skillful Soldiering for Contentment

Having prepared daily over a long period of time to live Today for the glory of God, you have to go out and actually fight the battle. Soldiers in every era of history have trained for years to hone their skills for future battles. Medieval English archers began training as early as seven years of age, and by the time they took the battlefield, their chest muscles were thick from years of repetitive practice. But all that training is worthless if they don't ever take the field, or if they disregard the patterns for skillful shooting they have developed to prevent them from firing wildly during the battle. So it is with Christian contentment. We have to train ahead of time and then put into practice the skills we have learned to fight for contentment.

Practice the Presence of Christ. In your daily quiet time, you should have already reconnected with Christ as the vine and yourself as the branch. You now need to live that out moment by moment. The Captain of your soul will lead you by the power of the Spirit into battle against discontentment. He will make you alert to Satan's devices and empower you to fight. So, by the Spirit, "abide" in him continually. Apart from him, you cannot be content. As this or that circumstance comes up, be mindful of the fact that Christ "will never leave you nor forsake you" (Heb. 13:5) and that he has already promised to filter your temptations so that Satan cannot overwhelm you with a test too strong for you to withstand (1 Cor. 10:13).

Throughout church history, godly people have written on "practicing the presence of the Lord." A Roman Catholic monk named Brother Lawrence wrote the most famous of these books in the seventeenth century: *The Practice of the Presence of God.* As a monk, he had been assigned to a menial job in the kitchen. But he did these small acts of service while conscious of the continual presence of a great God. The issue was not the greatness of the tasks but the motive behind doing them.[6] As Paul said, "Whether you eat or drink, or whatever you do, do all to the glory of God" (1 Cor. 10:31).

Practicing the presence of Christ allows us to turn simple daily tasks into heavenly gold, not unlike the fairy-tale character Rumpelstiltskin, who could spin straw into gold. The Puritans who lived out what scholar J. I. Packer called "reformed monasticism" knew this idea well: without withdrawing to some retreat center or cloister surrounded by high walls, we could live a life continually focused on God but still out in the hustle and bustle of a normal existence in the world.[7] They practiced the presence of Christ while carrying on their trades or their farming or their housekeeping.

Pray Continually. Part of abiding in Christ is continual prayer. This is different from the extended prayer time you should have in your morning quiet time. Rather, it is the kind of moment-by-moment immediate prayer displayed by Nehemiah when he prayed silently and quickly before asking the king for resources to rebuild the wall of Jerusalem (Neh. 2:4–5). Paul commanded this in 1 Thessalonians 5:17: "Pray without ceasing."

This is a powerful tool in continual Christian contentment. When the circumstances are annoying or irksome, lift them up to Christ and ask him to give you patience. When a massive trial hits, cover it immediately in prayer. When Satan tries to sever you from the vine, to cut off the flow of nourishing sap that flows from your Savior, defy him by increasing your prayers. Pray in bumper-to-bumper traffic; pray when changing a tire in the pouring rain; pray when you've fallen ill all weekend with a stomach virus; pray when praised by someone for a generous action on your part. Pray at all times with all kinds of prayers and requests (Eph. 6:18). By this alone will you defend your citadel of contentment from the devil's relentless attacks.

Give Thanks in All Circumstances. Immediately after telling us to "pray continually," Paul commands us to "give thanks in all circumstances, for this is the will of God in Christ Jesus for you" (1 Thess. 5:18). It is obvious how closely related continual thankfulness and contentment are. The common verbal link of "all circumstances" and "in any and every circumstance" (Phil. 4:12) is a dead giveaway. Being able to look at all things as good reasons for thanksgiving is the essence of the doctrine of providence applied to actual daily life. Learn to thank God for inanimate objects that seem to be demon possessed, like a stack of dishes that comes spilling out of the cabinet, or a door that bounces back into your face as you're trying to walk through, or a computer that freezes up just when you need it to function smoothly. One of Jonathan Edwards's resolutions is relevant here: "Resolved: Never to suffer the least motions of anger toward irrational beings."[8] If we should thank God even for the tiniest moments of our lives, how much more for the massive, earth-shaking events as well—like the death of a spouse. As we have seen, in her grief, Sarah Edwards thanked God when Jonathan died. George Mueller, who ran orphanages that cared for over ten thousand orphans in nineteenth-century England, did the same at the passing of his wife.[9] Both Edwards and Mueller remembered God's kindness in allowing them to have their spouses for as long as they did. Thankfulness is a powerful antidote to discontentment.

Starve Sin to Death by Killing Specific Temptations. The basic handbook on spiritual warfare in sanctification is Romans 6–8. I will not walk through those rich verses carefully here,[10] but I want to make a few assertions based on them. First, as Christians, we have been decisively moved from the realm of sin and death (in Adam) into a new realm of righteousness and life (in Christ). The person we were born into in Adam is dead, spiritually crucified through Christ. We have been given a new identity in Christ, and on that basis we are set free forever from sin (Rom. 6:11, 18). What that means is that we need never sin again; no temptation will ever come to us with authority and have the right to demand that we yield to it. What that means for contentment is that we can put to death every single temptation toward complaining, toward bitterness and sourness, toward rebellion against the wise and fatherly disposal of God. We can by the Spirit kill all of these temptations, every single one of them (8:13)!

Though we cannot finally kill any sin pattern (like complaining) so that we know it will never trouble us again, we can gradually weaken that habit by starving it to death. As Paul put it in one key verse, "We know that our old self [i.e., who we were in Adam] was crucified with him in order that the body of sin might be *brought to nothing* [Greek, *katargeō*: rendered progressively weaker], so that we would no longer be enslaved to sin" (Rom. 6:6). The old person we were in Adam is dead forever; the body of sin will be with us till the day we die, but we can gradually weaken it by starving it. We starve it by killing off specific temptations toward discontentment by the power of the Spirit, learning new habits of contentment. In the end, this is how a formerly bitter, sour, habitual complainer can learn the secret of being content in any and every circumstance and become a consistent delight to be around.

Set a Guard over the Door of Your Mouth. A great deal of our resolve to be content in any and every circumstance leaks out of our mouths once trials come. We bleed out our joy and spiritual power in a series of words that ought not to be said. Psalm 141:3 says, "Set a guard, O LORD, over my mouth; keep watch over the door of my lips!" We must not allow sinful words of unbelief and filthy complaining to escape our lips. My home is not far from a maximum-security federal prison in Butner, North Carolina. Imagine the terror to our community if those prisoners managed to escape and flood into our streets! So it is with words of complaining. When Sarah Edwards heard about the death of her beloved Jonathan, she said, "O that we may kiss the rod, and *lay our hands on our mouths.*" Remember this lesson as we've unfolded it in chapter 9. Our mouths should speak the faith that fills our hearts: "God is sovereign; he is loving. Everything that happens to me, he has ordained. All of this will end in his glory and my salvation. To God be the glory!"

Be Quiet and Slow Things Down. Sometimes we fly off the handle and react quickly before we've had a chance to ponder and reflect and take a deep breath. We need to slow things down and see what God is doing. Second Peter 3:8 says, "With the Lord one day is as a thousand years." That is an amazing concept! God sees everything in super slow motion, and every microsecond of history is calculated and part of God's providential plan. Don't let Satan speed things up. Slow down! Breathe! Quiet yourself under God's mighty hand (1 Pet. 5:6).

Exercise Your Faith. Christian contentment is completely based on a faith perspective, the ability to see what is invisible. Faith is the eyesight of the soul, by which we see invisible spiritual realities, past, present, and future.[11]

We have to see the *past* with eyes of faith: God's majestic plan of redemption from Adam's fall until now; Christ's atoning death for us; his resurrection from the tomb; his ascension to heaven.

We have to see every *present* spiritual reality with eyes of faith: the invisible God seated on his heavenly throne; the invisible Christ at the right hand of God, interceding for us and ruling the world; the invisible Holy Spirit indwelling us, moving throughout the world, executing God's plans for his children.

We have to see the *future* through eyes of faith: Judgment Day, in which we will give God a meticulous account for everything we have said or done in any and every circumstance; second, heaven, in which all these painful trials will have worked in us a weight of glory that far outweighs them all.

This is what we have faith in, these realities of what has been, of what is, and of what will be. But like a muscle, faith grows stronger with use. When we meet particularly challenging circumstances with Scripture and prayer rather than with carnal anger or frustration, our faith is exercised as we think about the past, the present, and the future. This greatly glorifies God.

Recite Memorized Scripture. The spiritual discipline of Scripture memorization is a powerful weapon in daily life for maintaining a contented outlook. I have already advocated Scripture memorization as a daily spiritual discipline. Now, at the moment of battle, when Satan is assaulting your soul with temptations and accusations, you must wield the mighty sword of the Spirit, which is the Word of God (Eph. 6:17).

Special Projects to Build Contentment

As a final feature to develop our skills and strength in Christian contentment, let me advocate some very practical actions. These will not require much explanation but, if put into practice, may strengthen you greatly as you pursue this excellent goal.

Study the Heroes of Church History. Hebrews 11 in its Hall of Faith catalogs the men and women whose lives of faith stand as timeless examples for those who would run the Christian race after them. They are those "of whom the world was not worthy" (v. 38). They wandered in deserts and mountains, in caves and holes in the ground. They were poverty-stricken and persecuted.

The annals of the church since the days of the apostles have continued this record. Study those who braved the terrors of barbarian tribes to bring them the gospel. Study those who crossed snow-clogged mountain passes to reach a new people in the valley beyond.[12] Study the imprisonment and execution of the Roman martyrs,[13] the courage of those who cared for the sick during the Black Death,[14] the boldness of Luther at the Diet of Worms,[15] the chronic and painful illnesses of John Calvin,[16] the self-sacrificial courage of women like Gladys Aylward,[17] Amy Carmichael,[18] and Elisabeth Elliot.[19] Zero in especially on how they suffered and what they said about it—how, for example, God overcame Adoniram Judson's depression after the death of his wife and daughter in Burma.[20]

Realize the dark and light threads of providence that God has woven for twenty centuries. As you compare your life to theirs, be humbled, be convicted, and be inspired. Their stories should make us ashamed to complain of minor afflictions, or even major ones. And they will teach us how to act when it is our turn to shine.

Study the Persecuted Church. Some of these stories are unfolding in our time as well. We have much continual information available about the persecuted church in various places in the world, of brothers and sisters in Muslim and Communist nations who are imprisoned or beaten for their faith by government officials. We also know of places in North and East Africa where lawless bands of Muslims roam around burning churches and slaughtering Christians.[21] Go to the websites of ministries like Voice of the Martyrs, Persecution Project, and Open Doors[22] to learn more. Let their accounts move you to prayer and action. Let them also humble you and make you less likely to complain.

"Hold the Ropes" for Missions. As we saw above, this is the striking image William Carey used for people supporting his bold missionary work with finances, prayers, and many other encouragements. Beyond merely studying church history and the persecuted church, immerse yourself more and more in the cause of the spread of the gospel to the unreached peoples of the world. Though you may not be called to go as a career missionary yourself, you can and should "hold the ropes" for those who are. This involves adopting some missionaries as a focus, reading their prayer letters, communicating regularly with them (through email, Skype, and other instant communication apps), supporting them financially, and perhaps even going on short-term mission trips to encourage and help them in their work. Your increased sacrifice for the global cause of Christ will help you grow in Christian contentment as you care less and less about the frivolous things of modern Western culture.

Fast Periodically from Specific Worldly Pleasures. Fasting is a powerful discipline to expose idolatries of the heart. Paul says of all lawful pleasures, "I will not be dominated by anything" (1 Cor. 6:12). How can we tell if some worldly pleasure has gained mastery over our souls, thus opening up a bleeding wound in our contentment? Fasting is a prime diagnostic and a powerful remedy. And though we usually think of fasting as only in reference to food, we can fast from Netflix, NFL games, golf, recreational shopping, specific comfort foods (chips, ice cream), social media, video games, and other such things. Spend the freed-up time in reading and prayer for supernatural contentment in your soul.

Get Involved in New Ministries That Will Stretch You. There are many ministries that have tremendous power to stretch your faith and cause you to grow in godliness. The more challenging they are to your "creature comforts" and worldly concerns, the better they can purge you of discontent. Get involved in pro-life causes, including working with crisis pregnancies. Or join a ministry that helps regions affected by natural disasters (hurricanes, earthquakes, tornadoes, tidal waves). Go on a short-term mission trip to an impoverished city in the developing world. Or get involved in the refugee crisis by helping at a resettlement center in Europe or the Middle East. How about volunteering at an urban rescue mission working with people recovering from addictions? Or working for racial reconciliation through legal advocacy for at-risk teens? These experiences have transforming power, enabling you to rub shoulders with Christian brothers and sisters who are further along in Christian contentment than you are. You will learn how much of the world suffers and that the bubble of protection afforded by our wealth is unreal and not conducive to the development of true Christian contentment.

Seek Avenues of Service That Are Thankless. Every church or ministry has servant roles that will afford almost no spotlight. Regularly embrace these kinds of service. Learn to serve thankless people, developing a remarkably mature ability to derive secret joy from pleasing an invisible Lord with not a single earthly reward.

Visit the Elderly, the Sick, and the Dying, and Comfort the Bereaved. Ecclesiastes says, "It is better to go to a house of mourning than to go to a house of feasting, since that is the end of all mankind, and the living should take it to heart" (7:2 CSB). The same book of wisdom says, "Remember also your Creator in the days of your youth" (12:1). It is certainly a much more powerful lesson in Christian contentment to minister day after day to an elderly or even a dying person than to go to parties celebrating the success of some sports team. As we look into the shockingly changing visage of a dying person, a person we once knew as robust and active as we are now, it is a sobering lesson on the future all of us will have in the grave. The selflessness that comes from meeting the continuous needs of a bedridden loved one is a supernatural stroke from the Master Sculptor to shape our souls. While it may seem harsh, when we go to a funeral and look into the lifeless face of the corpse, our faithless views of life in this world can lose their power.[23] And when we hear the sobs of the family as they recount the many ways this woman or man blessed their lives, we realize how brief is life in this world. Having officiated many funerals as a pastor, I realize how impossible it is to capture a life in a few words of eulogy. All that really matters is praise from the Lord in heaven: "Well done, good and faithful servant" (Matt. 25:21).

When a Financial Windfall Comes, Give More Than Ever. Wealth is often an idol and can be devastating to true Christian contentment. When extra money comes, pray about giving more of it away than you ever dreamed you would. Let regular patterns of sacrificial giving be a weapon to kill the love of money that is the root of all kinds of discontentment (1 Tim. 6:10).

Seek Accountability and Prayer Support for Contentment. Ask your spouse, your children, your parents, your pastors, your small group members, your accountability partners, your discipler/disciple, your fellow church members, your Christian coworkers two questions: (1) Do you see any regular patterns of discontent in my life? (2) Will you pray for me to grow in Christian contentment in any and every circumstance?

Make Contentment a Regular Feature of Family Life. It is vital for husbands and wives to be deeply content with each other, lest they stray into infidelity. Guard your hearts in your marriage; pray with and for your spouse in this area. Also incorporate lessons of Christian contentment into your regular family devotions with your kids and as you meet individually with your children for discipleship.

Read Books on Contentment, Providence, and Suffering. The Jeremiah Burroughs book we've used as a guide throughout this study, *The Rare Jewel of Christian Contentment*, is one of many Puritan Paperbacks put out by Banner of Truth Trust. Read Burroughs's book, as well as the similar study by Thomas Watson, *The Art of Divine Contentment*. Also study such titles as Watson's *All Things for God* and John Flavel's *The Mystery of Providence*. On the issue of pain and suffering, Richard Sibbes's *Bruised Reed* and C. S. Lewis's *The Problem of Pain* are helpful. John Piper's *Desiring God* is the best book that I've ever read on seeking pleasure in God alone.[24]

Beware the Danger of Continual Internet Accessibility.
Every generation of Christians has had to fight Satan's complex masterpiece, "the world" (1 John 2:15–17), with its lusts, allures, praises, pleasures, and values. But the digital age we live in has generated some powerful electronic delivery systems capable of pouring worldliness into our eyes every single instant. Be vigilant that your smartphone, tablet, and other electronic toys are not tools of Satan to work constant discontentment in you. These devices are showing a terrifying power to make us restless and impatient, with very short attention spans. They make us long for things we cannot have and show us incessant images of things that may well already be idols for us. Ask the Holy Spirit to show you how your electronic devices, especially your smartphones, are making you discontent.[25]

A Final Word: This Is a Lifetime Work

The secret that the apostle Paul said he learned was paid for with the greatest catalog of suffering in the history of the Christian church. We should not imagine our growth in Christian contentment will come without a cost to us.

Jeremiah Burroughs ends his book with this point: Christian contentment is very hard to win. It is easier to preach sermons on it (or write books about it) than to actually learn it and live it. He compared it to the difficulty of bridling the tongue, which James says is evidence of being a perfect man (James 3:2). Burroughs wrote of a man who fixed his soul on one verse of Scripture: "I will take heed to my ways, that I sin not with my tongue" (Ps. 39:1 KJV). That man focused on it every single day, and later he testified, "I have been these thirty-eight years learning this lesson, and have not yet learned it thoroughly." Although that lesson may be difficult, Burroughs said, learning contentment is even harder.[26]

As hard as it is, and as costly as the tuition for Christ's school of contentment is, few subjects of the Christian life will pay as many sweet dividends, both in this life and in the next. It is worth it to pursue this rarest of jewels for the rest of your lives, dear friends, and to see how God uses you to speak hope to the hopeless of this world. When you display a practiced skill and supernatural strength of Christian contentment in any and every circumstance, you will be infinitely wealthy in eternity and lead a host of transformed people into heavenly glory behind you.

Notes

Chapter 1 A Rare Jewel in a Discontented World

1. "Moussaieff Red," Smithsonian National Museum of Natural History, accessed July 30, 2018, https://geogallery.si.edu/10026485/mous saieff-red.

2. This refers to *Doctor Faustus* (1604) by Christopher Marlowe. Mephistopheles is a Satan-like figure who makes a deal for the soul of Dr. Faustus. Many times people in our age speak of someone "selling his soul to the devil" for some earthly benefit. The devil tricks the individual into some arrangement that he later bitterly regrets.

3. Gregg Easterbrook, *The Progress Paradox: How Life Gets Better While People Feel Worse* (Chicago: Random House, 2004).

Chapter 2 Paul Teaches the Secret of Christian Contentment

1. The word is *autarkēs*, from *autos* (self) and *arkeō* (to be enough or sufficient).

2. Italics that appear in Scripture quotations have been added for emphasis.

3. Wayne Grudem, *Systematic Theology* (Grand Rapids: Zondervan, 1994), 160.

4. John Piper, "I Believe in God's Self-Sufficiency," *Trinity Journal*, n.s., 29 (2008): 227–28.

5. C. S. Lewis, "The Weight of Glory," *Theology*, November 1941, http://www.verber.com/mark/xian/weight-of-glory.pdf.

Chapter 3 The Definition of Christian Contentment

1. "History of the Hope Diamond," Smithsonian, accessed July 30, 2018, https://www.si.edu/spotlight/hope-diamond/history.

2. Jeremiah Burroughs, *The Rare Jewel of Christian Contentment* (Carlisle, PA: Banner of Truth, 2013), 19.

3. Burroughs, *Rare Jewel*, 19.

4. A. A. Milne, *Winnie the Pooh* (New York: Puffin Books, 2005), 72.

5. Burroughs, *Rare Jewel*, 21.

6. Andrew M. Davis, *An Infinite Journey* (Greenville, SC: Ambassador International, 2014), 37.

7. James Dobson, *When God Doesn't Make Sense* (Wheaton: Tyndale, 1993), 61–62.

8. Justo L. Gonzalez, *The Story of Christianity* (San Francisco: Harper & Row, 1984), 1:46.

9. Burroughs, *Rare Jewel*, 21–22.

Chapter 4 Contentment and Providence

1. "Inside the Manufacture with A. Lange & Söhne," YouTube video, 5:56, posted by Hodinkee, April 16, 2015, https://www.youtube.com /watch?v=07JOiZOKVR0.

2. Wayne Grudem's definition of providence: "God is continually involved with all created things in such a way that he (1) keeps them existing and maintaining the properties with which he created them; (2) cooperates with created things in every action, directing their distinctive properties to cause them to act as they do; and (3) directs them to fulfill his purpose." Grudem, *Systematic Theology*, 315.

3. Kara Rogers, "Biosphere 2," Encyclopedia Britannica, September 23, 2011, https://www.britannica.com/topic/Biosphere-2.

4. Richard Sibbes, quoted in I. D. E. Thomas, *A Puritan Golden Treasury* (Carlisle, PA: Banner of Truth, 1997), 229.

5. "For Want of a Nail," Love Poems, accessed July 30, 2018, http://www.love-poems.me.uk/childrens_nursery_rhymes_for_want_of_a_nail.htm.

6. Roland Bainton, *Here I Stand: A Life of Martin Luther* (New York: Abingdon-Cokesbury, 1950), 34.

7. Bruce Gordon, *Calvin* (New Haven: Yale University Press, 2009), 64.

8. D. Bruce Hindmarsh, *John Newton and the English Evangelical Tradition* (Grand Rapids: Eerdmans, 2001), 13.

9. Arnold Dallimore, *Spurgeon: A New Biography* (Carlisle, PA: Banner of Truth, 1995), 18–20.

Chapter 5 The Mysterious Mindset of Contentment

1. Burroughs, *Rare Jewel*, 41–85.
2. Burroughs, *Rare Jewel*, 42–43.
3. William Barclay, *The Secret of Contentment* (Philipsburg, NJ: P&R, 2010), 97–108.
4. Carl O'Donnell, "The Rockefellers: The Legacy of History's Richest Man," *Forbes*, July 11, 2014, https://www.forbes.com/sites/carlo donnell/2014/07/11/the-rockefellers-the-legacy-of-historys-richest-man /#3300b30c3c26.
5. "John D. Rockefeller," New World Encyclopedia, last modified May 15, 2018, http://www.newworldencyclopedia.org/entry/John_D._Rockefeller.
6. Andrew M. Davis, *Isaiah: Christ-Centered Exposition* (Nashville: B&H, 2017), 260.
7. Burroughs, *Rare Jewel*, 51.
8. Tim Ellsworth, "Kurt Warner's Hall of Fame Career Defined by Faith," Christian Index, August 10, 2017, https://christianindex.org/war ners-hall-of-fame-career-defined-by-faith/.
9. James Joyce, *Portrait of the Artist as a Young Man* (New York: Penguin Classics, 2003), 127.
10. John Wesley, journal entry for December 23, 1755, in *The Works of John Wesley* (Grand Rapids: Baker Books, 2002), 2:352.

Chapter 6 How Christ Teaches Contentment

1. Burroughs, *Rare Jewel*, 19.
2. In the KJV, Mark 14:33 accurately records that Jesus was "sore amazed," as though he was experiencing something shocking. The word translated "amazed" is *ekthambeomai*, which is often used for the stunned reaction of the crowd to one of Jesus' miracles.
3. Burroughs, *Rare Jewel*, 128.
4. Melvyn Goh, "Ancient Secrets: The Forbidden City," Pilot Guides, accessed July 30, 2018, www.pilotguides.com/articles/ancient-secrets-the -forbidden-city.
5. Francis Chan, *Forgotten God: Reversing Our Tragic Neglect of the Holy Spirit* (Colorado Springs: David C. Cook, 2009), 107–8.

Chapter 7 The Excellence of Christian Contentment

1. Burroughs, *Rare Jewel*, 120.
2. In my book *An Infinite Journey*, I argue that God has set before every Christian two infinite journeys—the internal journey of spiritual growth toward Christlikeness, and the external journey of evangelism/

missions. The stages of salvation are regeneration, justification, sanctification, and glorification. *Infinite Journey*, 17, 39–54.

3. Burroughs, *Rare Jewel*, 128.

4. William Wilberforce, quoted in Christopher D. Hancock, "The 'Shrimp' Who Stopped Slavery," *Christian History*, January 1, 1997, https://www.christianitytoday.com/history/issues/issue-53/shrimp-who-stopped-slavery.html.

Chapter 8 The Evils and Excuses of a Complaining Heart

1. Burroughs, *Rare Jewel*, 137.

2. Burroughs, *Rare Jewel*, 137.

3. Burroughs, *Rare Jewel*, 138.

4. Burroughs, *Rare Jewel*, 185–206.

5. Courtney Anderson, *To the Golden Shore: The Life of Adoniram Judson* (New York: Dolphin Books, 1961), 378. Judson was not suicidal but morbidly introspective. He dug his own grave and sat by it as an act of self-denial, seclusion, and meditation. He wrote at that time, "God is to me the Great Unknown. I believe in him, but I find him not."

Chapter 9 Contentment in Suffering

1. John Wesley, journal entry for January 25, 1736, in *The Works of John Wesley*, 1:21.

2. Wesley, journal entry for January 25, 1736, 21.

3. Wesley, journal entry for January 25, 1736, 21.

4. God used the experience with the Moravians to show Wesley that he did not have a genuine faith in Christ. So when Wesley returned to England, he sought counsel from some Moravian brothers, especially a man named Peter Böhler. Wesley formed a religious society with him, and they met at Aldersgate Street in London. On May 24, 1738, at a meeting of that society, Wesley had his evangelical awakening: "I felt my heart strangely warmed. I felt I did trust Christ, Christ alone, for my salvation." Wesley, journal entry for May 24, 1738, in *Works of John Wesley*, 1:103. See also Iain Murray, *Wesley and Men Who Followed* (Carlisle, PA: Banner of Truth, 2003), 8, 37.

5. Timothy Keller, *The Reason for God: Belief in an Age of Skepticism* (New York: Dutton, 2008), 23.

6. David Bentley Hart, "Tremors of Doubt," *Wall Street Journal*, December 31, 2004, quoted in John Piper, *A Sweet and Bitter Providence: Sex, Race, and the Providence of God* (Wheaton: Crossway, 2010), 26.

7. C. S. Lewis, *Mere Christianity* (New York: Macmillan, 1960), 31.

8. C. S. Lewis, *The Problem of Pain* (New York: Macmillan, 1973), 14.

9. Lewis, *Problem of Pain*, 81.

10. See Tertullian, *Apologeticus*, chap. 50, in *Ante-Nicene Fathers* (Peabody, MA: Hendrickson, 1995), 3:55.

11. Sarah Edwards to Esther Edwards, April 3, 1758, quoted in George Marsden, *Jonathan Edwards: A Life* (New Haven: Yale University Press, 2003), 495.

12. William Shippen to Sarah Edwards, March 22, 1758, quoted in Marsden, *Jonathan Edwards*, 494.

13. John Piper, *Don't Waste Your Cancer* (Wheaton: Crossway, 2011).

14. This is an amazing picture of Christ's substitution for us.

15. It was from C. S. Lewis that I first learned this idea of the humility of God in accepting us back after we have tried idols and been left empty by them:

> Let me implore the reader to try to believe, if only for the moment, that God, who made these deserving people, may really be right when He thinks that their modest prosperity and the happiness of their children are not enough to make them blessed: that all this must fall from them in the end, and that if they have not learned to know Him they will be wretched. And therefore He troubles them, warning them in advance of an insufficiency that one day they will have to discover. The life to themselves and their families stands between them and the recognition of their need; He makes that life less sweet to them. I call this a divine humility because it is a poor thing to strike our colours to God when the ship is going down under us; a poor thing to come to Him as a last resort, to offer up "our own" when it is no longer worth keeping. If God were proud He would hardly have us on such terms: but He is not proud, He stoops to conquer, He will have us even though we have shown that we prefer everything else to Him, and come to Him because there is "nothing better" now to be had. (*Problem of Pain*, 85)

Chapter 10 Contentment in Prosperity

1. Burroughs, *Rare Jewel*, 227.

2. "Over 70% of all Christians are of Dalit and tribal communities, and the average Hindu associates the gospel with the underclasses of their society." Patrick Johnstone and Jason Mandryk, *Operation World: 21st Century Edition* (Carlisle, UK: Paternoster, 2001), 312.

3. Cotton Mather, quoted in Leland Ryken, *Worldly Saints: The Puritans as They Really Were* (Grand Rapids: Zondervan, 1990), 63.

4. "Mission Stats: The Current State of the World," The Traveling Team, accessed September 14, 2018, http://www.thetravelingteam.org/stats.

5. David B. Barrett and Todd M. Johnson, *World Christian Trends AD 30–AD 2000: Interpreting the Annual Christian Megacensus* (Pasadena, CA: William Carey Library, 2001), 551.

6. Randy Alcorn, *Money, Possessions, and Eternity* (Wheaton: Tyndale, 2003), xi.

7. "Definitions," Joshua Project, accessed July 30, 2018, https://josh uaproject.net/help/definitions.

8. "Mission Stats: The Current State of the World," The Traveling Team, accessed September 14, 2018, http://www.thetravelingteam.org/stats.

9. Timothy George, *Faithful Witness: The Life and Mission of William Carey* (Birmingham: New Hope, 1991), 74.

10. Lewis, *Problem of Pain*, 44.

11. David W. Jones and Russell S. Woodbridge, *Health, Wealth and Happiness: Has the Prosperity Gospel Overshadowed the Gospel of Christ?* (Grand Rapids: Kregel, 2011), back cover.

12. Jones and Woodbridge, *Health, Wealth and Happiness*, 15.

13. Alcorn, *Money, Possessions, and Eternity*, 299.

14. For more on the fund-raising for the Metropolitan Tabernacle, see the excellent account in Lewis A. Drummand, *Spurgeon: Prince of Preachers* (Grand Rapids: Kregel, 1992), 345–47.

15. R. G. LeTourneau, *Mover of Men and Mountains* (Chicago: Moody, 1967), quoted in Ed Hird, "R. G. LeTourneau: Model of Generosity," North Shore News, accessed September 14, 2018, http://www3.telus .net/st_simons/nsnews019.html.

16. John Wesley said, "Money never stays with me. It would burn me if it did. I throw it out of my hands as soon as possible, lest it should find its way into my heart." Quoted in Randy Alcorn, *The Treasure Principle* (Colorado Springs: Multnomah, 2001), 70.

Chapter 11 Contentment Is Not Complacency

1. Richard Baxter, *The Reformed Pastor* (Carlisle, PA: Banner of Truth, 2007), 67–68.

2. Jonathan Edwards, "Resolutions," in *A Jonathan Edwards Reader*, ed. John E. Smith, Harry S. Stout, and Kenneth P. Minkema (New Haven: Yale University Press, 1995), 274–78.

3. David Brainerd, journal entry for November 4, 1742, in *The Life and Diary of the Rev. David Brainerd*, ed. Jonathan Edwards, in *The Works of Jonathan Edwards*, vol. 2 (Peabody, MA: Hendrickson, 2000), 329.

4. J. Hudson Taylor, *A Retrospect*, 3rd ed. (Toronto: China Inland Mission, n.d.), 119–20, quoted in John Piper, "The Ministry of Hudson Taylor as Life in Christ" (message, Desiring God 2014 Conference for

Pastors, February 5, 2014), https://www.desiringgod.org/messages/the
-ministry-of-hudson-taylor-as-life-in-christ.

5. George, *Faithful Witness*, 18.

6. Anderson, *Golden Shore*, 354–78.

Chapter 12 How to Attain and Protect Contentment

1. Burroughs, *Rare Jewel*, 41.

2. Malcolm Gladwell, *Outliers: The Story of Success* (New York: Penguin, 2008), 38–76.

3. Gladwell, *Outliers*, 61.

4. George Mueller, *A Narrative of Some of the Lord's Dealing with George Muller, Written by Himself, Jehovah Magnified. Addresses by George Muller Complete and Unabridged,* vol. 1 (Muskegon, MI: Dust and Ashes, 2003), 271.

5. I wrote a booklet on how to memorize chapters and books of the Bible: Andrew M. Davis, *An Approach to the Extended Memorization of Scripture* (Greenville, SC: Ambassador International, 2014).

6. Brother Lawrence of the Resurrection, *The Practice of the Presence of God*, trans. Sister Mary David, SSND (New York: Paulist Press, 1978).

7. J. I. Packer, *A Quest for Godliness: The Puritan Vision of the Christian Life* (Wheaton: Crossway, 1990), 28.

8. Edwards, "Resolutions," 275 (#15).

9. In his autobiography, George Mueller wrote of his wife Mary's death in a chapter titled "Kissing the Rod," the exact expression Sarah Edwards had used in her grief. Mueller preached at Mary's funeral, using as his text Psalm 119:68: "You are good and do good." He had three main points: (1) God is good and did good to bring Mary into his life to begin with; (2) God is good and did good to allow Mary to live with him as long as she did; (3) God is good and did good to take Mary home to heaven when and how he did. George Mueller, *Autobiography of George Mueller* (Denton, TX: Westminster Literature Resources, 2003), 431.

10. I give a careful exposition of Romans 6–8 in *Infinite Journey*, 48–52.

11. Davis, *Infinite Journey*, 134–40.

12. Ruth Tucker, *From Jerusalem to Irian Jaya: A Biographical History of Christian Missions*, 2nd ed. (Grand Rapids: Zondervan, 2004).

13. W. H. C. Frend, *Martyrdom and Persecution in the Early Church* (New York: New York University Press, 1967).

14. In 1527, Martin Luther wrote a treatise in which he sought to strengthen the faith of those who stayed where the bubonic plague was raging. Martin Luther, "Whether One May Flee from a Deadly Plague,"

in *Martin Luther's Basic Theological Works*, ed. Timothy Lull (Minneapolis: Fortress, 1989), 736–55.

15. Bainton, *Here I Stand*, 167–89.

16. These bodily problems included gout, cyclical fevers, migraine headaches, intestinal problems, gallstones, coughing up blood, etc. See Gordon, *Calvin*, 278–79.

17. Janet Benge and Geoff Benge, *Gladys Aylward: The Adventure of a Lifetime* (Seattle: YWAM Publishing, 1998).

18. Elisabeth Elliot, *A Chance to Die: The Life and Legacy of Amy Carmichael* (Old Tappan, NJ: Revell, 1987).

19. Elisabeth Elliot, *The Savage My Kinsman* (Ventura, CA: Gospel Light, 1981).

20. Anderson, *Golden Shore*, 378–87.

21. Nik Ripkin, *The Insanity of God: A True Story of Faith Resurrected* (Nashville: B&H, 2013), 103–8; Voice of the Martyrs, *I Am N: Inspiring Stories of Christians Facing Islamic Extremists* (Colorado Springs: David C. Cook, 2016); Mindy Belz, *They Say We Are Infidels: On the Run with Persecuted Christians in the Middle East* (Carol Stream, IL: Tyndale, 2016).

22. https://www.persecution.com; https://www.persecutionproject.org; https://www.opendoorsusa.org.

23. Jonathan Edwards seized the opportunity afforded by the shocking death of a teenager in Northampton to warn all at the funeral how quickly life can end. Basing his comments on Psalm 90:5–6, which likens human life to grass that flourishes in the morning but withers by evening, he spoke of how this young man was recently the picture of health, vigor, and youthful beauty. "How those countenances that were most beautiful and delighting to beholders while there was life and heath become unpleasant and loathsome to the sight by death. Their beauty consumes away like a moth." Edwards warned his hearers not to squander their lives in sin, but to be ready at any moment to die and stand before God. See Marsden, *Jonathan Edwards*, 154.

24. Thomas Watson, *The Art of Divine Contentment* (Carlisle, PA: Banner of Truth, 1986); Thomas Watson, *All Things for Good* (Morgan, PA: Soli Deo Gloria, 2001); John Flavel, *The Mystery of Providence* (Carlisle, PA: Banner of Truth, 1998); Richard Sibbes, *The Bruised Reed* (Carlisle, PA: Banner of Truth, 1998); John Piper, *Desiring God: Meditations of a Christian Hedonist*, rev. ed. (Colorado Springs: Multnomah, 2011).

25. Tony Reinke, *12 Ways Your Phone Is Changing You* (Wheaton: Crossway, 2017).

26. Burroughs, *Rare Jewel*, 227.

Andrew M. Davis is pastor of First Baptist Church of Durham, North Carolina, and a visiting professor of church history at Southeastern Baptist Theological Seminary. Chairman of the governance committee of The Gospel Coalition (TGC), Davis has written articles for TGC's popular website and has spoken in plenary and breakout sessions at TGC's national conference. He is the author of *Revitalize* and *An Infinite Journey*, named by Tim Challies as one of the top ten books of 2014.

Also Available from
ANDREW M. DAVIS

"I can't recall ever making this statement about a book: **CHURCH LEADERS NEED THIS.**"

—THOM S. RAINER, president and CEO, LifeWay Christian Resources

TWO
JOURNEYS

Helping Christians Make Progress

Sermons — Classes — Podcasts — Bible Studies

www.twojourneys.org

Advocate for Gospel-Centered Principles and Practices

To learn more, visit:
www.TheGospelCoalition.org